Erika's Amerika

26 delightful essays documenting a Greek family's adventures and adaptation to life in America.

Compiled and written by
Kristalenia Spyratos

Kristalenia Spyratos

Kristalenia Spyratos holds a
Master's Degree in Education
from Northern Illinois University.
She has written several essays on education
and is currently Director of Studies at a
Foreign Language School in Kefalonia Greece.
This is her first book of short essays.
She also happens to be Erika Analitis' daughter.

Erika's Amerika

Kristalenia Spyratos

Erika's Amerika
is available for purchase at our online bookshop
www.fast-print.net/store.php
and from leading Worldwide online bookshops
including amazon.com

FastPrint Publishing
www.fast-print.net/store.php

Erika's America: Second Edition

A catalogue record for this book is available from the British Library

ISBN 978-178456-097-3

First published 2014 by
FASTPRINT PUBLISHING
Peterborough, England.

An environmentally friendly book printed and bound in England by
www.printondemand-worldwide.com

FSC Mixed Sources
Product group from well-managed forests, and other controlled sources
www.fsc.org Cert no. TT-COC-002641
© 1996 Forest Stewardship Council

PEFC Certified
This product is from sustainably managed forests and controlled sources
www.pefc.org
PEFC/16-33-415

This book is made entirely of chain-of-custody materials

Typeset in 12pt. on 16pt. ITC Berkeley Book

All of the essays in this book are based on actual events.
Some of the names have been changed
in the interest of privacy, protecting our friends
who made so many memories possible.

For Mana

In life,
it is not the destination that matters,
but the journey leading there.

Acknowledgements

Thanks to all our customers over the years
and a special thanks to Diane Boyer
for her unending memories.

Erika's America
by Kristalenia Spyratos
edited by Anastasia Analitis-Genc

Design, Typesetting,
Imaging & Output Files
prepared for digital printing
by Denis Jordan

The author and publisher wish to thank Wendy Doremus for allowing the use of one of her late husband's photographs on page 151, for which, sadly, he paid the ultimate price. Bill Biggart's unique collection of spectacular photographs depicting the horrific events of 9/11/01 can be seen at Bill's official website:- www.billbiggart.com

The author and publisher would like to thank the following sources for their kind permission to reproduce the pictures on page 89: www.allurelimo.com and on page 151: www.billbiggart.com

Contents

Prologue

In the early seventies, many European immigrants packed their bags, and their dreams, to head for a land called America. America was a place that promised freedom, democracy and hope for a better future through education and economic prosperity. One of those people was Erika Analitis, a Greek immigrant from a tiny village on the island of Kefalonia in the Ionian Sea. Erika, along with her husband and two children, made the long trek across the Atlantic, like so many others, in the hope of giving their children more than they had. They brought with them all of their Greek ideals and values not knowing any other way of life. The things Erika experienced in America would transform her into the person she is today. She had a mind that was open enough to toss out the outdated do's-and-don'ts of her generation and to assimilate to this wondrous new place and its sometimes strange ways. For Erika, the American dream took on new meaning, sometimes for the better, other times for the worse. One thing is certain, the life experiences she had, could have happened in no other place.

The Big Move

Erika held tightly onto her son's small and pudgy hand and her husband clutched their two-year old daughter in his arms as they passed through customs. The airport was like nothing she'd ever seen, especially since she had never been inside of one before that day. Hundreds of people were hurriedly bustling about carrying heavy and cumbersome suitcases, jockeying for a better position in line, or tearfully hugging their loved ones and wondering when they would see them again. The Athens airport was tiny in 1972; that was the year that Erika and her family made the move to America. Her husband, Tasso, had made the decision despite her protests.

When Erika and Tasso got married in 1965 Tasso

said that they would leave Greece in search of a better life in Germany. Erika didn't want to leave her homeland, but she finally consented in the end, as was proper for Greek women of that generation. Erika and Tasso moved to Germany shortly after their wedding and they were not alone. Many of their friends and relatives also made the move and they all lived close to each other. Erika and her husband worked in factories because neither of them had more than an elementary school education growing up in a small fishing village on a tiny island in the Ionian Sea in the '40s and '50s. Besides that, a deal struck between the governments of Germany and Greece allowed residents of Southern European countries to emigrate to Germany but only allowed for resident status permitting manual labor in Germany's industrial district, with essentially no other rights normally bestowed to immigrants. The good thing was that they worked only eight hour days, five days a week. On the weekends they would visit with relatives and enjoy the city of Düsseldorf like the locals. In Germany, life was good. However, Tasso didn't want to settle for a life of menial jobs, raising average kids who would also eventually work menial jobs. Tasso aspired to own his own business instead of toiling a lifetime away to make someone else rich. After the birth of their second child, Tasso decided to take his family to America where they could realize the American Dream.

Looking around Chicago's O'Hare airport, Erika

was awed, and a bit overwhelmed. It was huge! There were lines of people everywhere, snaking around valet ropes. People were scurrying through them, like mice in a maze, to get their passports checked, collect their luggage and pray that they didn't need to have their suitcases searched. Thousands of people were speaking hundreds of different languages, wearing brightly colored clothes and strange hair styles. There were enormous signs painted with arrows pointing to corridors that seemed to be never-ending. It was like the American films that they used to watch on German TV. Erika silently prayed that everything would go well during their entry into this strange and wondrous country. She felt comfort in knowing that her brother was waiting outside to drive them to her father's house. Erika's parents, sister and two brothers had moved to the states a few years before them, and her father had filed the necessary paperwork to sponsor her family's immigration into America.

After clearing customs, using the little English that her husband knew, they collected their four tattered suitcases, which contained everything that they owned in the world, and headed for hope. Erika's brother was waiting on the other side of the exit and they found him in bell-bottom jeans and a huge afro standing proudly in front of the most gigantic car they had ever seen. It reminded Erika of those huge funeral cars that she had seen in the movies. During the ride to their new home she took in all the sights; rows of identical cookie-cutter homes, assorted shops lining the streets one after another, exhaust-belching buses crowded with people, and taxis being driven by impatient cabby's who were perpetually blaring their horns. This was, after all, Chicago. Erika couldn't believe the size of the expressways with their wide, paved lanes stretching past the horizon; the incredible number of cars and trucks, and mile-after-mile of exits to God-only-knew-where.

They arrived at her parents' apartment complex twenty minutes later and when they pulled up next to the building, Erika was amazed at the size of it. They would only stay there temporarily, but it was comforting for her to be with her family since everything in this country was new and very different from Germany. Erika saw her mother standing in the doorway with a broad smile on her round face and a shimmer of joyful tears in her eyes for the reunion with her daughter. Erika rushed to embrace her and wrapped herself around her mother so tightly that she thought they might never be separated from each other. Erika felt like a child in a new school who didn't want to go to class, and Tasso was the class bully. Her mother reassured her that everything would be okay, and Erika looked at her husband with resentment for bringing her to this place.

Tasso smiled and said to her in Greek, "Here, we make our lives better."

Erika hoped, for his sake, that he was right.

The Relocation

The time came for Erika and her husband to move their family into an apartment of their own, which was located two blocks from her parent's. She had begun adjusting to her new surroundings quite well and life was finally stable. She and her husband were working in factories again and they had lots of family nearby. Almost everyone they knew from their village, of their generation, seemed to have ended up in Chicago too. That was the trend with immigrants; the braver ones would venture off to somewhere new and then they would write to tell the others if it was worth their while to do the same. Sometimes, even if the decision was disastrous, they would talk it up anyway so that they didn't have to suffer alone. Aside from the fact that Erika worked nights, things were running smoothly.

Her husband worked days so babysitting, fortunately, was not an issue for them. Erika tended to the kids until five o'clock when she would have to leave for work.

Working those odd hours wasn't without its adventures. Upon returning home one crisp October night at around 2:30 am, Erika found a skinny little nine-year-old girl, with short tangled brown hair and a thin, world-weary face, curled-up asleep on the steps outside of their apartment building. Erika was shocked, and for a minute she didn't know what to do. 'My God!' she thought. It was very late but she couldn't possibly leave the girl there. She thought of what she would want someone else to do if they found her child sleeping somewhere out in the cold. Erika knocked on the door of a neighbor who lived in the apartment next to hers. The woman opened the door looking groggy, with sleep lines on the left side of her face, smudged mascara leaving black semi-circles under her eyes, and a tattered old robe hanging sloppily from one shoulder.

"What's going on?" the woman yawned in a deep, sleep-induced raspy voice.

It was obvious that the woman was a bit peeved, and since Erika spoke almost no English, she quickly motioned to the woman to follow her and pointed to the sleeping child. The neighbor shook her head and ran her fingers through her tangled hair and simply said, "Not again." Erika stared at her unable to understand.

"Her Mom's got a new boyfriend and he don't like kids, or at least he don't like this one, and you know she's a drunk anyway. I'll take her in with me tonight." She said on a grunt as she lifted the child into her arms and disappeared through her apartment door.

Erika caught the word 'boy' and wondered if the woman was drunk, since it was obviously a little girl. Erika breathed a sigh of relief knowing that someone was looking after that poor child and she went up to her apartment to sleep. She wondered what in the world could possible cause a parent to forget their child was not home?

The next morning Erika told her husband what had happened upon her return home from work the previous night.

"The people are different here." he answered between sips of coffee, totally uninterested.

He figured that it was none of their business anyway. They came here to better their own lives, not the neighbors' lives.

I couldn't tell what the woman was saying in English, "I have to learn the language better." Erika mumbled to herself.

Tasso sat for a moment, lost in thought when he finally declared, "You're right. Tomorrow I'll go and register for English lessons at the junior college." Erika merely rolled her eyes and congratulated Tasso on his decision.

Car Trouble

Greeks have always respected money and the benefits of always having a stash set aside for 'just-in-case' situations. Times were sometimes tough in Chicago, but Erika and her husband managed to get by. Erika made more money than Tasso ($106 per week to his $93) and Tasso, being the head of his household, could not stand for this. His Greek ego was entirely too big to let his wife out-earn him. So, to supplement his income, Tasso began working as a waiter at a nearby banquet hall whenever they needed and extra set of hands. A Greek friend who worked there was able to get him the job. It was tiring work to run the gauntlet of tightly packed banquet tables carrying fifty pound trays of food and praying that no out-of-control kid tripped him as he passed, but he was being paid in cash so it was worth it.

Since he had been making some extra money, Tasso decided to go out and buy a cheap old car. It was a 1963 Chevy Corvair the color of lilacs with a black vinyl interior that you could lose flesh on in the heat of summer. He was very proud of his purchase; after all he got it for a steal. He pulled up to his apartment building, honked the horn and waited for his family to come down and see what he got for them. When Erika and the kids finally came out to see what the all commotion was, Tasso propped one leg up on the open door's panel, leaned back on the car, spread a mischievous grin on his face and said,

"Isn't she a beauty?"

Erika knew the look on his face all too well. It was the look of the cat that ate the canary. Nonetheless, she was pleased at the idea that they could now go to places other than work.

A few months passed and one Tuesday afternoon, while Tasso was driving home from work, the car began to sputter and jerk, and suddenly smoke began billowing from the engine compartment at the rear of the car. He was nearly home and was able to push it into a spot on his street with the help of a few of his cousins. This new development explained why the car was so cheap. Tasso propped open the hood and began examining the engine. He scratched his head trying to figure out what could be wrong with the car. Of course he didn't know the first thing about cars, but that didn't really seem to faze him. Three days later the city put a sticker on the windshield warning that the car would be towed if it was not moved within twenty-four hours. Since Tasso and Erika didn't have the money to repair it, they just left it right where it was.

That Saturday morning, Erika was making breakfast for the family since she had the weekends off. Her son George was sitting in front of the living room window watching some of the older neighborhood boys play kickball in the street.

"Yoryi, (George in Greek) come and have some breakfast. Kris, you too." Erika called to the kids in Greek.

Her daughter promptly peeled herself away from *The Brady Bunch* and sat at the kitchen table, but George didn't budge.

"Yioryi! Come for breakfast."

"In a minute Mana" George said.

He was sitting at the window with his chin propped in his hands leaning against the window sill when he saw a tow truck pull up. The driver of the truck asked some of the neighborhood kids if they knew who the car belonged to but the kids paid him no attention. The driver shrugged his shoulders and, per city orders, proceeded to tow the car. George's eyes grew to the size of saucers and he raced to the kitchen and said, ***"Momtheyaretakingourcar!"***

Erika looked at him in surprise and said,

"What? Slow down and say that again."

George drew a breath and said more calmly,

"There is a man in a truck out there and he is taking our car!"

They both rushed to the window, with Kris excitedly following on their heels.

"Look!" George said pointing out the window to a spot down the street.

Erika quickly pulled her son from the window. She knew that they would have to pay a fine so she told her son to be quiet so the driver wouldn't hear him. She took George back to the kitchen and hoped that no one would come knocking on the door looking for the car's owner. When Tasso came home Erika told him what she saw. He looked at her with a half-amused crooked smile and reassured her that there was no problem because the car was in someone else's name, he had already removed the license plates and it was a piece of junk anyway. Tasso was very clever, even if he was somewhat ethically challenged.

More Car Trouble

That wasn't the only time that Erika and Tasso had car trouble. Tasso had lived through an economic depression so he learned to be a very frugal man. He never took a price at face-value, always thought that people were trying to rip him off, and was forever looking for a 'great deal'. So it didn't come as a surprise that the next car he bought was also crap. It was a mint green 1964 AMC Rambler with a dark grey cloth interior. It was obvious that the previous owners got their money's-worth, but that didn't leave much life in it for Erika and her family. Of course no one will ever know how long that car might have lasted since it ran into a bit of trouble that had nothing to do with engine failure.

Tasso parked this car in the alley behind the

apartment building since it was easier to exit through the back porch of their unit. One Sunday afternoon, the family had returned home from having lunch at Erika's parent's house, who lived only two blocks away. Tasso went to take a nap, the kids plopped themselves in front of the television and Erika was in the kitchen mending yet another hole in George's jeans. It was a quiet afternoon and a light spring breeze was blowing through the apartment's open windows. Erika was thinking about how nice things were and that maybe things would go well here in America.

She had barely finished her thought when she heard voices chattering away from the alley outside. The voices started to get animated and began multiplying, as if a crowd was gathering. Then the voices became louder and started sounding a bit panicked, and suddenly sirens could be heard in the distance. Erika went to the window to see what all the hubbub was about. What she saw made her gasp. Their car was on fire.

"Tasso, Tasso! The car's on fire, wake up!" she yelled in Greek.

Still sleepy, and more than a little annoyed at being disturbed, Tasso muttered...:*W-w-what?*"

"***Get up!*** The car is on fire. The police and the fire department are downstairs!" Erika screamed in alarm.

Tasso jumped out of bed and ran to the window. All he could say was "Oh my God!" He quickly went downstairs and approached a policeman.

"What's heppen? This my car!" Tasso demanded in his thick Greek accent.

"Calm down sir, the fire department has already put out all the flames." replied the officer.

Some older women were giving statements to the police while pointing to a group of young boys. Apparently, the boys thought it would be a lot of fun to throw a lit match into the car through a partly open window, which caused the upholstery to catch fire. Even though the fire didn't reach the engine, the car's interior was charred beyond recognition, leaving the car worthless. Tasso began slowly shaking his head in disbelief and cursing under his breath about what kind of parents could raise children that do this kind of thing, and where he thought those parents should go. Erika watched the events from the apartment window and she couldn't believe this was happening. The boy who owned the matches stood with his head hung low and Erika watched, stunned, as the boy's father grabbed him from the shoulder and started to pound on him. Tasso tried to intervene but the police stopped the beating first. The boy's father refused to take responsibility for the damages and since it was not the youngster's first offence he was hauled off to jail. Erika feared for her children's future. Would she be able to discipline them in this jungle that they moved to? Would her influence triumph over all of the outside pressures, like television and other children, which could certainly sway her kid's sense of morality?

For a moment she couldn't even breathe from the idea that the answer might be no.

Sleepless Nights

Erika's kids had to find ways to entertain themselves because being poor didn't allow for luxuries. Since they had only their imaginations, Erika's kids were quite creative, unlike many kids today. They devised their own fun without fancy dolls or an Atari game console. They would build elaborate forts using only bed sheets and chairs, or they would stick an old tennis racket between the couch cushions like a gear shift, and use a cheap Frisbee as a steering wheel and pretend that they were in a car racing adventure. Sometimes they simply chased each other around the apartment and made Erika and Tasso crazy.

One night Erika was working her usual night shift at the Zenith television factory and came home around midnight. She was dog-tired and couldn't wait to take a nice steamy shower and turn in. She quietly tiptoed through the house trying not to wake anyone. She made her way to the bathroom and, upon opening the bathroom door, she almost stepped on her little daughter who was fast asleep on the floor. Erika was puzzled, but she scooped Kris up and put the little girl back into her bed. She returned to take that shower she was so longing for, but as she reached for a towel something plopped onto the floor with a smack. She looked up to see where it came from and noticed what looked like dozens of tiny carnations stuck to the ceiling of the bathroom. At first, she couldn't figure out what they were but upon closer examination she realized that they were dried balls of tissue.

The next morning at breakfast Erika asked her children what they did the night before. The answer was the usual. Their dad fed them, they watched TV, and then he put them to bed. Looking to her little girl Erika asked,

"What did you do last night sweetie?"

"I slept." The little girl replied not looking up from her bowl of Corn Flakes.

"Nothing else?" Erika asked, raising an eyebrow.

"Oh, I had to go pee." Kris replied with a mouthful.

"All you did was pee?" Erika tried to coax the story from her daughter.

The child thought for a minute and finally responded,

"Only pee, no poop." Erika pursed her lips and closed her eyes so that she didn't lose her patience.

"What did you do after you peed?"

"I made flowers." Kris smiled proudly.

"How did you do that?" Erika asked, though she thought that she already knew the answer.

Excitedly, Kris went into detail about how she took the tissues from the box, dunked them into the toilet, since the sink was too high, and threw them up to the ceiling. She said it was a good thing that the ceiling was slanted or they wouldn't have made it, which explained the ones on the floor. Erika couldn't help but laugh at how proud her four-year-old was of her disgusting accomplishment. She was just thankful that she kept a clean toilet. Erika spent most of the morning peeling and scraping the 'flowers' off of the bathroom ceiling, all the while wondering how much toilet water her daughter had drunk.

Home Alone

For Erika, being a good Mom meant making sacrifices for the good of her children. Every day Erika walked her son George to and from school. This was a big city and it was unsafe to let the boy go with the neighborhood kids, after all, he was only six and spoke limited English. Erika had heard the horror stories of kidnappings and accidents that happened while kids were crossing the big roads. One blustery, snowy Chicago winter day, the time had come for Erika to pick her son up from school. The temperature was hovering around freezing, the wind was whipping around wildly and the snow was coming down thickly. Erika's daughter was sleeping and she thought it would be a shame to wake her and subject her to this awful weather for a ten minute round trip walk. The school was only two blocks away and she would be back with George in no time. The little girl had only been asleep for twenty minutes, so what were the chances that she would wake up anyway? Erika quietly locked the door and took off as fast as she could in the direction of the school. The snow was so bad it blurred her vision and the wind felt like a wall blocking her way. She ducked her head and plowed through and thought to herself that it was better she hadn't woken her daughter.

On the way back she told George, "Hurry honey, we have to walk faster. Our little Kris is home alone."

Erika gripped her son's hand and hurried him along. Erika could see the apartment around the corner and thought "Two minutes and we'll be home." She started to have an uneasy feeling in the pit of her stomach, probably mother's intuition, and urged little George to walk even faster. She realized that when she decided to leave her daughter home alone she hadn't considered that maybe the phone would ring or some other noise in the apartment might wake her up. As they hurried closer, she looked up to her apartment window only to see a most agonizing sight; little Kris, with her nose pressed to the bedroom window, crying her heart out. Erika's heart sank. What had she done? Kris was crying so hard that she had reached the point of the silent cry; the cry that is so heart-wrenching that you can't even catch your breath. These were the times that Erika most resented the decision to move.

She and her son raced up the stairs, George's little head bobbing back and forth as his Mom tugged at him to go faster so they could get to the frightened child. Erika flung the door open in seconds, all the while telling her daughter she was right there. She ran to Kris, fell to her knees and pulled her daughter into a tight embrace trying to console the sobbing child. It took her a good fifteen minutes to calm Kris down and try to explain why she wasn't there when she woke up.

"Oh, don't cry my love, Mommy is here. I just went to school to pick up Georgie. You know how we go every day. But today you were asleep and I didn't want to wake you. I'm back now, don't cry."

She cursed herself for leaving the child alone and vowed to the little girl that she would never leave her again. For the next few days, Erika's daughter fought to stay awake until it was time to go get her brother from school lest she be left alone again.

A few days later, while walking with Kris to pick George up from school, Erika looked down at her little girl and wondered how much future therapy the girl would need to deal with issues of abandonment. She quickly shook off that thought with a chuckle. It was a good thing that Greeks didn't believe in silly stuff like psychology.

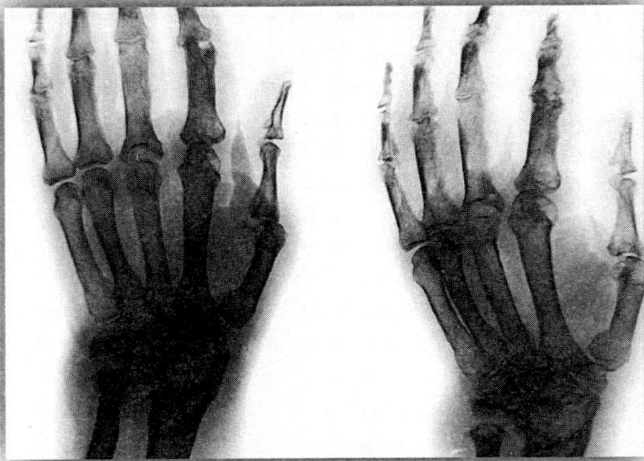

Overworked!

Erika's work ethic was quite strong because she was raised to believe that if you worked hard you got ahead in life. Erika worked in the Zenith television factory and she was content in her job. She was paid a standard salary but could receive bonuses depending on how many units of plastic knobs she produced during her shift. She worked with a diverse group of women comprised of many ethnic origins like Greeks, Polish, Germans, Mexicans and African Americans. Many of her coworkers were immigrants just like her. Having been taught that strong work ethic by her father (who felt that whoever didn't want to work could starve) Erika worked as hard as she could. She was in her mid-twenties, healthy and able-bodied, however since she spoke very little English, she relied on a Greek co-worker for translations and a general heads-up on what was going on.

One night, while she was diligently working at her post, one of the Mexican women, along with an African American, woman grabbed her hands and told her to slow down. Erika looked up in puzzlement and raised her eyebrows signaling "What?" The African American woman spoke louder and slower, as if Erika was deaf instead of foreign.

"You need to slow down 'cause we ain't gonna bust our asses to keep up with you. The quota is 100. What's up with you? Slow down. You making us look bad."

Erika could tell the women were annoyed, but she really didn't understand why. She searched the room for her Greek friend Ria. Ria hurried over when she heard the woman raise her voice.

"What's the matter ladies?"

"She gotta slow down. She goin' too fast. What she tryin' to prove?"

Ria turned to Erika and explained what they were saying. Erika was stunned that anyone would ask her to work at less than top speed, and she got annoyed.

"What? Ria, I need to make some extra money, I don't want to slow down."

Ria frowned. "You don't understand. These women have been here for a long time. I don't know what they might do if you don't ease up."

Erika sighed. She couldn't believe this. The land of the free? Ha! She thought. Erika was quiet for a minute then she looked up and said,

"Ria, tell the manger I want to see him."

"Are you crazy? You can't tell the manager that they don't want to work! They'll get fired and who knows what they'll do to you."

"No, no. Tell him I want to be moved to a post by myself."

Days later, Erika was moved to an individual post. She and Ria came up with the excuse that Erika couldn't read in English so she couldn't keep up. It was the only excuse they could think of which wouldn't make the other workers think that they were being betrayed. The manager, who was not an idiot himself, had realized that something was amiss when Erika's production suddenly went down, and he agreed without asking questions so as to not cause a ruckus among his employees. He didn't care where she worked, as long as she worked as hard as she had before. The harder she worked, the better he looked anyway.

During her breaks, Erika would sit with her English-Greek dictionary trying to learn the language, determined to understand what the people around her were saying. For someone with only an elementary school education, this was not easy. It didn't help that all the women she sat with were Greek and spoke in their mother tongue. The ladies from the other departments would walk by and Erika felt as if they were boring holes into the back of her head with their glares as they passed.

Erika thought to herself,

"So much for the land of equal opportunity."

My House, My Rules

Discipline is very important in Greek households. Children are taught to respect, obey and learn from their parents. Back in the day (and the old country), many parents used corporal punishment to keep their kids in line (it could probably do some good in this day and age too). Erika didn't like to hit her kids and rarely ever found the need to spank them. She felt that taking away things that they wanted, like TV, was much more effective.

When Erika and her family moved to Chicago, many well-intentioned relatives wanted to help them get adjusted. They explained to the newcomers about customs, rules and regulations, and the laws regarding children. One afternoon, while having coffee at a cousin's house, Erika learned about how strict the laws were when it came to child-rearing. Her cousin was talking about the mandatory attendance at school and how parents had to phone in when kids were sick to inform the school. In the village there were about sixteen kids and all of their houses were within 150 feet of the school, so the teacher pretty much knew who was or wasn't in attendance. Erika's cousin continued,

"Oh, and don't think that you can spank your kids in this country." Erika was dumbfounded.

"What?"

"Yes Erika, you can't hit the kids. If you do, they can call the police and then the state will take them away from you for abuse."

Erika couldn't believe that the state could meddle in her home life. While she thought that hitting kids was not the best way to handle them, she was not against an occasional spanking on the bottom for outright defiance. Later that evening, after dinner, the kids were doing their homework and Tasso was watching the evening news. After cleaning up the kitchen, Erika sat on the couch next to her husband.

"You know, Ekaterina told me something interesting today."

Tasso raised an eyebrow showing only mild interest.

"What was so interesting?" he responded, barely turning away from the television.

Erika went on, "She said that, in this country, we can't spank our kids."

This got Tasso's attention and he actually started laughing.

"Really and why is that?"

Erika tried to get him to be serious.

"Apparently it is illegal to spank kids in this country, and if we do, the kids can call the police and the state can take them away from us."

Erika waited for his response. He turned to her with a look of total disbelief and with a crooked grin said,

"No one, no matter where we are, is going to tell me how to raise my kids. They are mine to do with as I see fit."

With that, he got up and called for the kids to come into the living room.

The kids came in and asked what he wanted.

"Sit down." said Tasso in his 'you're in trouble' voice. George and Kris sat down looking at each other puzzled, and a bit worried, since they hadn't done anything wrong… that they could recall. Tasso paced back and forth in front of where the kids sat with his hands on his hips. He began his lecture (always in Greek so they would not forget their roots).

"It seems that this country is very different from our own. They have laws which, outside the house, we all must obey."

The kids were even more confused now, maybe

their dad was going to jail for breaking the law they thought, a bit frightened.

"You're both too young to know this but, in Greece, a man's home is his own. This means that he sets the rules and he ***alone*** enforces them. So, just in case your friends at school tell you that your parents can't yell at you or spank you, know that they are ***wrong.*** In this house ***I*** am the police. You will ***not*** call them for anything except an emergency like a fire."

Tasso then bent down very close to their scared little faces and, in a cold and low voice said,

"Don't even think about calling the police if I raise my hand to you, because you will surely have done something to deserve it, and I will cut your tiny little fingers off before you can even dial. Understood?"

The kids both quickly nodded in agreement and figured that a little slap was not worth losing limbs.

"Okay, go back to whatever you were doing."

Erika was shaking her head in stunned silence as her kids scurried back to their room whispering to each other. Erika turned to Tasso and said with irritation in her voice,

"You know you have good kids who never disobey you. Weren't you a little hard on them?"

"I know, but just in case, let them be warned. Kids can easily be influenced by their friends." he said.

As she thought about what had just happened, Erika decided that she was glad that she did all of the disciplining; she only threatened the kids that she would tell their father on them to scare them. After Tasso's speech, she figured she probably wouldn't even have to take things away anymore. Ironically, Tasso never did hit the kids. Ever.

The Wild West

For families just starting out, first homes are not always what they dream of. Erika's was a second floor, two bedroom apartment on the west side of Chicago on Walton Street. For some reason, one of the bedrooms (the kid's) didn't have a door. Since they couldn't afford to replace it, Erika had hung some beaded curtains. It was, after all, the 70's. The bathroom was minuscule and it was located under a set of stairs, so you had to bend while showering. The kitchen was also small but it was comfortable. There was room for a small table and it had counter space for food preparation. As unremarkable as the apartment was, it had one interesting feature; some very eccentric neighbors downstairs.

On several occasions, Erika and her husband could hear screaming voices coming from downstairs, along with slamming doors and breaking glass. They tried to ignore the disturbing sounds but sometimes things would get really out of control.

Late one spring night, after the kids had long gone to bed, Erika and Tasso were watching the late night news. The announcer had just finished a story about a violent shooting in Chicago, which wasn't as common back then as it is today.

"I can't imagine what would make someone just pull out a gun and shoot another human being." Erika said to Tasso.

Tasso shook his head in agreement.

"This is a whole different place. People just don't seem to respect each other here."

Erika wasn't really listening. She was thinking about how safe the village was back in Greece. Everyone knew each other and no one would ever think of harming a fellow human being. She was still reminiscing when the screaming from downstairs came floating through the floor boards. The man was drunk again and he was yelling at his girlfriend. She screamed back at him and soon doors started slamming and glass started breaking. The force of the slamming doors was so great that Erika could feel it reverberate under her feet. At times like these Erika was grateful that her kids were heavy sleepers.

Tasso was fed-up with the fact that these screaming matches were a frequent weekly occurrence and suggested that he should go downstairs to tell them to shut up. Erika quickly dissuaded him.

"You don't know what state of mind that man is in or how many people are down there. Are you crazy?"

She was amazed at what the woman downstairs tolerated. Erika believed that no man had the right to talk to his wife that way; although her grasp of English vocabulary was far from perfect, she like most foreigners had learned many of the more colorful expletives and their respective meanings. Her own father never raised his voice to her mother, nor did Tasso ever yell at Erika or speak to her with such disrespect. Tasso would raise his voice to make a point, but the guy downstairs was being downright vicious. Erika didn't speak English that well, but she caught the words 'fucking bitch' many, many times.

Tasso was about to turn up the volume on the television to drown out the noise, when the voices downstairs seemed to finally go still. Tasso and Erika looked at each other thinking that perhaps that would be the end of the fighting for the night. Suddenly a loud POP shattered the silence, and they were shocked into attention once again. What they heard was a gunshot.

"Oh my God! He's going to kill her!" Erika screamed as she ran into the kid's room to see that they were okay. That's when they heard the second shot.

Tasso jumped up from the couch and picked up the phone, but hesitated about calling 911. He didn't know what the consequences would be for his family if he got involved in someone else's troubles. Erika ran back into the living room and said,

"They're still sleeping. What are we going to do? What if the bullets come through these wooden floors?!" She pleaded with her husband, "Let's take the kids and go to my father's house, please!"

Tasso decided to call the police. This situation was now endangering his family, so to-hell with the consequences. He told his wife to go in the kids' room in case they woke up. The call to 911 connected and, in broken English, Tasso told the police his address and about the situation downstairs and then he sat by the door waiting for them to arrive. The screaming continued and two more shots rang out before the police arrived. Tasso went to the edge of the stairwell to hear what the police were saying. He wondered if the police would give him up as the caller. Tasso could hear the calm voices of the police officers and then the drunken ramblings of the couple. He was telling the cops to 'mind your own fucking business' and she was sobbing and pleading not to take her abuser away. After a bit of a scuffle, the police arrested the guy and locked him in their cruiser. They came back up to ask Tasso some questions but quickly dropped the interrogation when they realized he didn't speak English very well. Of course Tasso cleverly pretended he didn't speak any English at all so he wouldn't have to get any more involved than necessary.

As the sad story always goes, the guy was back a few days later and the cycle began anew. Until the day they moved out of that apartment, Erika stored all of their extra stuff under the kids' beds… just in case.

Sick Days

Erika felt that things in this country were very similar to her life in Germany. A factory job was a factory job anywhere you did it. That view changed one day when she got sick. She was suffering from a bout of the stomach flu, which was going around as it does every winter. She didn't want to lose the day of work so she went in for her regular shift. Because she was ill, she had to make several trips to the restroom. The floor manager had taken notice of her frequent absences from the floor and became agitated. Halfway through the shift he went up to her to see what was going on and why she was slacking on the job. He called Ria over to translate.

"Tell him that I don't feel good but I can finish the

shift." Erika told Ria. After hearing the explanation the manager shook his head and told her to go home.

"We don't pay you spend your time in the bathroom."

He motioned for another worker to come take her place, spun on his heels and left. Erika was very disappointed. She had to call her husband to come and get her since, even if she had the nerve to get into a cab alone at night, she would have difficulty telling the driver where to go. Tasso called Erika's sister to sit with the kids so he wouldn't have to wake them.

When Tasso pulled up Erika was waiting for him on the factory's front steps. She got in the car with a look of sadness.

"You okay.?" he asked her.

"No. Where did you bring us? The directors in Germany were nothing like this. I'm sick, but I went in and did my job, even if I was a little slower today. But by the end of the shift I would have met the quota." she explained in Greek.

"That guy didn't even ask me if I was okay. He didn't care; he just wanted the line to keep moving. So rude. So blunt." She was really upset.

Tasso tried to reason with her.

"You know, that's his job. He has someone to answer to if things don't get done. You should have just stayed home."

"We need the money." she replied defeated.

“I can’t believe how unfeeling these people are.” Tasso patted her on the back reassuringly.

“Don’t worry. We aren’t going be here long. I didn’t uproot my family so far away from our country to make someone else rich. We’ll find a way.”

Erika didn’t know at the time that he already had a plan in the works.

Diner Days

In the old days, Greek women were taught to respect and obey their husbands and never talk back, even if they were the ones who were right. One day Tasso made an announcement to his wife.

"Erika, I'm buying into a restaurant in the suburbs. We're moving."

Erika's jaw dropped open and her eyes nearly bulged out of her head. Every time she felt a sense of stability, her husband wanted a change.

"Wha… where… what are you talking about?

She was still trying to absorb the shocking news. Tasso began to explain,

"Remember George Liotis from the banquet hall?"

Erika nodded.

"Well, there's a truck stop for sale in a town called Roselle in the west suburbs. We're buying it together."

Erika wondered what they knew about restaurants, they hadn't even gone to one, except McDonald's for the kids, since money was so tight.

"Anyway, our factory days are over. We need to be out of here by the end of the month so if you can bring some boxes home from Zenith, we could use them."

And that was that. Erika's husband had decided on another life change for them. Deep down she trusted his judgment, but she resented his lack of consideration for her opinion. But, like her mother often told her, "That's just how men are, don't argue." So Erika, with uncertainty, began once again to collect their things for yet another move.

Three weeks later they had packed up the car and made the thirty minute drive out to their new home, and the place that would ultimately make their American dream come true. But not without a few adventures along the way.

Erika looked around their new apartment, which was conveniently located above the restaurant they bought, and thought 'What a dump.' It had potential though. Erika agreed to buying the place (not that she really had a choice) because an apartment was built right above the restaurant and the kids would be close so they wouldn't need a sitter. That was an expense they couldn't endure, especially since they had borrowed money for the purchase of the business, and had to pinch every penny.

Despite being raised in a village, Erika's mother had taught her style and class. She turned the house into a home with what little she had. They only had a few pieces of furniture and a black and white television that she got at a discount from Zenith, the factory she worked at in Chicago. She didn't mind the lack of extravagances though; Tasso had told her that now that they owned their own business they would prosper. All the things they couldn't have in Greece, and couldn't afford in Germany, would soon come their way.

After a week of cleaning and preparing their house, getting the kids into the local schools and overall settling in, the time finally came for Erika to go to work as a waitress, something she'd never done before. She figured that she had served her father as a girl, and now her husband, so how different could this be? That was the moment when her lifelong adventure began.

The restaurant was small, like an old-time diner. The place had dark brown brick walls, dark faux brick linoleum floors and brass fixtures. It had a small but adequate kitchen, a long counter facing the kitchen with naugahyde stools that were bolted to the floor, and a few small two-seater tables. Erika still spoke almost no English, so her first day was quite an experience.

They had a young girl working for them who was first hired by the original owner. Tasso and Erika thought it would be good to have someone there who knew the ropes since this was their first venture into the restaurant industry. Lori was 16-years-old, five months pregnant and had left home so she was on her own. Erika and Tasso practically raised her too. Lori explained to Erika, as best she could, what was on the menu and how the place was run. On that first day, Tasso was in the kitchen with the other cook and Erika was in front serving.

Her first customer, ironically, was Greek. Erika didn't know that at the time, and he didn't let on. In a heavy Greek accent Erika asked,

"Ken I halp you?"

"I'll have two poached eggs in a cup." the man replied.

He had spoken very fast and all Erika caught was 'cup'. So she headed for the soups and brought the man a cup of chicken noodle soup. The man looked at her in confusion and pushed the cup towards her and repeated his order.

"I'd like two poached eggs in a cup." he said, nodding his head and raising his eyebrows to show something was wrong.

Erika didn't understand, so she went back to the soups and brought him a bowl of chicken noodle soup instead. Again, the man shook his head to sign 'no'. Erika wasn't sure what was going on as the man pushed the bowl away again. She headed towards the kitchen, unsure what to do, but the man flagged down Lori and explained things. Lori gave the order as Erika wondered "who eats eggs in a soup cup?"

That day was difficult, but Erika survived with Lori's help and a lot of sign language. Years later the man finally admitted, with a chuckle to being Greek. Remembering that first day, Erika didn't find his joke very funny at all.

Roselle 5-0

The law was not something to be reckoned with, and whenever Erika saw police cars, she knew it meant trouble. One morning before the lunch shift, Erika and Lori saw police cars pulling up across the street and into the restaurant parking lot. The lights on the patrol cars were flashing but the sirens were off. The officers got out of their patrol cars and were looking across Lake Street at a small dilapidated house. The police were talking on their radios and a crowd was starting to gather. Tasso came out of the kitchen and asked his wife in Greek,

"What's going on out there?"

Erika shrugged and replied, "I don't know."

Lori looked at Tasso and suggested that he go

outside and see what was happening since this event was interrupting the lunch rush. Tasso agreed and went outside to see what all the fuss was about. He had attended English lessons at a junior college in Chicago to help him communicate since neither he nor his wife spoke English when they moved. It was broken English, but he was able to get his point across.

Erika nervously watched from the window as her husband approached two of the officers. This was the closest they had ever gotten to the authorities. Life in the village was pretty tame, and in Germany they were in a good neighborhood and had never witnessed any disturbances. She quietly wished to herself that Tasso not get involved in anything. Tasso reached the officers at the entrance of the parking lot.

"Hi guys. What's heppening?"

The officers looked him up and down before answering.

"Who are you?"

"I'm Tassos. This my place."

Tasso turned and pointed to the building behind him.

"Oh, you work here?" The officer asked.

Before Tasso could correct him, the man continued,

"See, there's these two kids holed up in that house over there."

The cop pointed to the little house across the street and went on,

"They're both minors and we gotta get 'em out. Girl's Mom wants to press charges. Says the boy's no good. Got her in there against her will."

Tasso didn't catch everything but he got the gist of things. The officer waited for some reaction from Tasso. Erika couldn't imagine what Tasso could be saying to the police and was getting more nervous. The other officer eyed Tasso.

"You know this kid? Name's Wayne Cramey."

Tasso thought for a moment. He and Erika had acquired many regulars at the restaurant but Tasso couldn't put a name to the face. He figured since he wasn't sure who they were talking about he might as well give a diplomatic answer. Tasso replied,

"Ya, he's goot boy."

The officers turned away indifferently. One said to the other,

"Nothin's gonna happen here. I think we should go, let the other guys deal with this."

They looked at Tasso and said,

"See ya' man. If the other officers need something they can use your phone right?"

Since it was the seventies there were no cell phones. Tasso nodded,

"Ya shur."

What Tasso didn't know was that Wayne's dad was standing with the others gathered in the crowd. The man came up to Tasso and patted him on the back to get his attention.

"Hey Tasso."

"Hi Paul."

Paul was one of the first customers to introduce himself to Tasso and his wife. He came into the restaurant almost every day for his morning coffee.

"I heard what you said to the cops about my son. Thanks man. I don't know what I'm gonna do with him. The Mom's pissed. That's her standing over there."

Paul pointed to a very angry mother in the distance. Tasso realized it was a good thing he had said nothing else.

"Ees okay Paul. You know boys, they likeh the trouble. I go back inside. Goot lack Paul."

Despite the heavy accent, Paul understood.

Back inside, Tasso explained to Erika what was happening and who the boy in the house was. She wondered what kind of place they had moved to, where teenagers could do these things and parents couldn't control them. Where she came from, you never even spoke back to your parents. She wondered how her kids would grow up and how she would make them listen to her with all these outside influences.

Four hours later the police got the kids to come out, with the help of their parents, and promises of no legal consequences. The next morning Paul came in to Tasso's. He got his coffee from Erika and told her thanks for what her husband did for him. A little later Paul sat with his friends and told them the story. The news of the foreigner's support of Paul's son spread fast and the customers saw these new people in a different light. They had no reason to help, but they did anyway. The whole story boosted their standing in the community and they were soon considered 'good people'. From that point on they had the respect of the entire neighborhood.

Neighbors

Some time had passed and Tasso's restaurant had become a regular hang-out for the people in the neighborhood. Tasso bought out his partner in record time and it no longer was considered a truck stop. Tasso and Erika allowed the district school bus to turn round in their parking lot so their kids could go to better schools. This brought in some of the parents from down the block. The parents were grateful that in the cold Illinois winters, these people let their kids wait inside for the bus to come. The neighborhood was beginning to change. The area surrounding the restaurant was pretty much prairie lands and underdeveloped when Erika and her family arrived. But just two short years later, developers were building a new subdivision half a mile away. Tasso knew this would be good for business. They had hired some new girls to accommodate for the increase in business since the construction workers came in almost every day. One of the new waitresses was a girl named Karen. Karen was a sweet girl of barely eighteen. Erika felt she should have been in school instead of trying to make ends meet at a roadside diner in the boondocks. Erika thought about how unfair life was to some people. She herself never got a good education, having only finished elementary school. However, her parents did the best they could do for her. She regretted not being able to go to school, but in her generation girls just didn't go to school. For Greeks, it was customary for girls to marry in their teens for fear of being left an 'old maid'. Erika was going to make things very different for her daughter. She would work hard so Kris could go to school and become something and stand on her own two feet. Her daughter would not have to depend on anyone.

It was around this time, in the late 70's, when a new owner took over the used car lot next door to Tasso's. His name was Jim Walton. He was the macho, tough-guy type who wore a lot of gold chains, sleazy leisure suits in eye-watering colors, and slicked back his dirty brown hair with Dippety Do. He soon became a regular at Tasso's and Erika didn't like the look of him from the first moment he stepped through their doors, strutting around like he owned the place. He was loud and obnoxious and would look the girls up-and-down wantonly. Erika thought only Greek men did that. She couldn't always hear or understand what he was saying to his buddies, but she could tell by his expression that it was something dirty. That really pissed her off. Erika grew up in a house where women were respected. Her father never even swore in front of his wife or daughters. Besides Walton's leering, Erika noticed that he seemed to have his eye specifically on Karen. The girl was still a teenager for heaven's sake! What was this guy thinking? He just rubbed Erika the wrong way.

One afternoon, Erika saw Karen and Lori with their heads bowed close together, whispering and giggling. Erika could tell by their giddiness that they were talking about men.

"Whaat's going on geerls?" Erika asked. Karen burst out and said,

"Oh Erika, Jim from next door asked me out on a date!"

Erika frowned.

"You know how old he be?"

"Oh, so what? I'm almost eighteen you know." Karen said indignantly.

Erika thought to herself, 'I know, do you know!?' Even though she felt she had to play mother to these girls sometimes, she knew she had no place telling them what to do. She could only give them some advice and hope for the best.

Weeks of giddiness continued from the girls as

they talked about all the dates and dramas of Karen's relationship with Jim. Erika noticed he seemed even more pompous than before (if that was even possible). Jim would pat Karen's bottom when she walked by him while she was working, and Erika wanted to pat him on the head… with a frying pan! Walton also called repeatedly during Karen's shift, which had begun to annoy Tasso to no end as he watched his customers have to wait for her to serve them. He let it go for a while but eventually told her to keep her private life out of the restaurant.

Karen's bliss, however, was short lived. One day she came into work very down. Erika asked her what was wrong, or if she was sick. Without many words, Karen explained that she didn't want to see Jim anymore but he wouldn't leave her alone. She never really gave a reason why. Erika felt for the girl and held back the 'I told you so' that was playing on the tip of her tongue. She was just glad that the girl had wizened-up.

"Is okay. You no hef to see him no more if you don wanne to."

Karen sighed.

"I don't. But he keeps calling me and he won't leave me alone."

She seemed a bit afraid of the guy or what he might do. An hour later Erika answered the phone,

"Tasso's, ken I halp you?"

It was Jim wanting to talk to Karen.

"She busy now."

Erika slammed the phone down, unwilling to talk to him. Minutes later, sure enough, Jim came in for coffee.

"You stay heer." Erika said to Karen.

"Ken I halp you?"

"Just coffee." Jim said sharply.

He kept looking at Karen. He motioned for her to come over to him. She ignored it.

"You wanne something else?" Erika asked curtly.

"No."

After half an hour he gave up and left. Karen was almost in tears.

"He's not going to leave me alone." she said to Erika.

"You no talk to heem no more." Erika told her, thinking it was that simple.

Later that evening, after they closed the restaurant for the night and while the kids watched TV, Erika relayed the day's events to Tasso. He said he thought something was going on.

"Eh, he'll stop coming in. What self-respecting man chases a woman who doesn't want him? It's none of our business anyway." Tasso explained in Greek.

"But she's just a child and he's an old man. He's slimy and he should be ashamed of himself!" Erika was upset now.

"It's not our problem." Tasso reminded her.

"But she's our employee. How would you like it if someone approached our daughter and was twenty years older than her?" she asked.

"My daughter would know better." he said matter-of-factly.

"Now forget it, I'm watching the news."

He turned to the TV. Erika knew it wasn't over though. Jim wasn't going to give up on Karen that easily. Erika's mother had told her that men have big egos and don't give up that easily for anything, especially when they get rejected. She went to bed that night wondering what tomorrow would bring.

Over the next few days, the calls kept coming from next door and Erika kept insisting that Karen was busy. Jim Walton was being as persistent as ever. Since Erika couldn't answer the phone every time it rang, Jim managed to get Karen on the phone and she hung up visibly shaken and upset. Tasso noticed and was fed up. He thought, 'What a loser this guy must be, chasing after a little girl who doesn't want him, like she was the only woman on the planet.' But, his business came first. Some of Jim's friends were in the place that morning and they were trying to convince Karen to go talk to Jim which was making her quite distraught. So, when Tasso took his coffee break he approached them.

"Hi guys."

"Hey Tasso." they replied. "We were just talking to Karen."

"Yah guys. I don know what's heppen, but she is work and please tell Jim to leave heer alone. Is enough now."

"Yeah, okay Tass" the one guy said.

Tasso figured that was it. It was his place and at least here, the girl would be left alone.

The next day, Lori was serving the guys from next door. They told her Jim's reply to Tasso's request. She immediately got Erika and in a panic Lori said,

"Oh my God Erika. Jim said that… Oh, I can't even repeat it to you..." Lori respected Erika very much, since Erika treated her like family.

"He said 'that fucking Greek' is not going to tell him what to do. Erika, Tasso shouldn't have said anything."

Erika went back to the kitchen to tell Tasso. She was half laughing, half worried. She knew Tasso was tough. He was raised that way. His parents, especially his mother, had given him the biggest ego of all his ten siblings. In Greek, she relayed the message. She was watching to read his reaction.

"Oh yeah?" he said.

Tasso cocked his head and a crooked smile tugged one side of his mouth, but he was fuming.

"Okay."

Tasso worked through the lunch shift and came out to have his coffee. Erika watched her husband because she knew this was the proverbial calm before the storm. Tasso wasn't a violent man, but he stood up for himself and any cause he felt worthy.

"What are you going to do?" she asked.

"No one is going to tell me what to do, especially in my own house. I asked the guy nicely to leave her alone, now I'm going to be more firm." he said in Greek. With that, he got up and walked next door. He would later tell Erika the events that took place after Tasso walked into Jim's office.

"Hi Jim." Tasso said in a low, flat and cold voice.

"Can I help you." Jim replied.

"Yah Jim, I think is enough with Karen eh? She young and you don let her to work. Come on, leave heer alone." Tasso said calmly.

Two of Jim's friends were standing on either side of him waiting to see what would unfold.

"Piss off Greek. I don't give a flying fuck what you say."

Jim sat behind his desk and leaned back in his chair, looked at his guys and a cocky smirk spread across his thin lips. Tasso sighed, placed his fisted hands on his hips and, almost imperceptibly, shook his head. Then, out of nowhere, he lunged over the desk and grabbed Walton by the collar with both hands.

"Okay. I try to be nice but you don wanne to understend. You come to my place again, I keel you! You got et?" Tasso growled through gritted teeth.

The other two guys stood, immobilized by shock, with their eyes wide and their mouths open. They gasped but did nothing. They didn't expect this.

"Yeah, I got it." Walton choked out.

Tasso released him, turned around, and left. From then on, Tasso gained the reputation as a 'tough guy' and a member of the Greek mafia. The former, at least, was true.

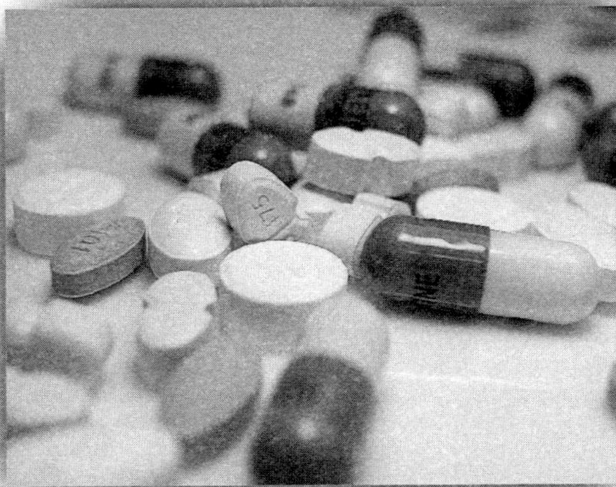

"Speedy" Service

The 80's rolled around and the time came to transform the diner into a full-fledged restaurant. Erika would have to deal with another Greek man, Tasso's brother, who was going to join the business. Since Erika and her sister-in-law had the same complaints about the brothers, they got along quite well. The restaurant would now seat about 80 customers, and would be open from six in the morning until ten at night, which meant more work.

Along with the new look came new customers which also meant new employees to cover the longer hours. One such employee was a woman named Sandy. Sandy had two kids around Erika's kids' ages, and lived only a few blocks away from the restaurant. She was a good person and Erika felt lucky that they had good people working for them. The closeness of the employees and the customers gave the place a homey feel. Everyone knew everyone, and also everything about everyone. Sometimes this was not a good thing.

Sandy worked hard. She had a lot of experience because, before she was actually hired, she used to hang out at Tasso's for hours at a time while her kids were at school. Her youngest child practically grew up in one of the high chairs. Sandy would help out by pouring coffee or serving orders if one of the other girls got really busy, all the while sipping her coffee and chatting with the other regulars. In fact, that's how she was offered the job. Erika told her that she might as well get paid for the time she spent in the restaurant.

Erika admired Sandy's stamina and wished she had the energy Sandy had. By the time Erika went upstairs to her apartment each night, she was wiped out. She had to make sure the kids had done their homework, taken their baths, were fed, had clothes ready for the next day, and she had to then straighten up any mess they might have made while they were unattended. Sometimes Erika wished she had a housekeeper. But of course, where she came from, it meant that you weren't a good housewife if you were unable to cope. Not to mention the fact that she couldn't afford that kind of help anyway.

One weekend it was Tasso's name's day. (Orthodox

Greeks celebrate the day of the saint that they were named after.) Erika had to work in the restaurant in the morning and then cook for the many relatives who would come over that night to wish Tasso well. Erika had already cleaned the house and had multiple ovens working in the restaurant's kitchen. The problem was that she also had a terrible toothache. Sandy noticed that Erika didn't look well.

"What's wrong?" Sandy asked her.

"I hef so much to do for toonight and my tooth hurts." Erika replied.

Sandy smiled devilishly and told Erika,

"I've got something that will help you if you want."

She proceeded to produce a bottle from her purse and offered Erika one of the little white pills. Thinking that it was an aspirin, Erika took the pill and downed it with a glass of water.

The night progressed and the guests started to arrive. Erika was busy greeting, serving, chatting and being an overall gracious hostess. She was amazed at the second wind she got after finishing her shift and going upstairs to begin the party. Her body seemed to almost hum. As the evening continued she cleared dishes, made coffee and served desert to over twenty five guests. At one point, her cousin Maria was talking to her but Erika's concentration began to waver and she couldn't register what exactly she was saying. Luckily Tasso came in to the kitchen, looking for a deck of cards, and interrupted the conversation and saved her.

After everyone had left, around two in the morning, Erika still felt energized so she started the cleanup she would normally have left for the next morning. While the rest of her family was sleeping she washed the serving dishes, swept and mopped the floor, and finally plopped down on the couch to unwind and watch TV. She wasn't sure what time she fell asleep, but it was close to dawn. The next morning she went to work and found Sandy having coffee at the counter.

"What was that peel you gave me yesterday? Sandy, my cousin was talken to me and I don even remember what she is saying to me!"

Sandy gave Erika a wink and smiled saying,

"It was good eh…"

It finally dawned on Erika how Sandy was able to be superwoman. Needless to say, Erika only took her own aspirin from that day forward.

Equal Opportunity Employers

There were times when, like most businesses, the restaurant was short staffed. These times were quite difficult for Erika, since she and Tasso had to do double shifts that sometimes totaled up to seventeen hours, now that the restaurant was open from six a.m. to ten in the evening. Because of the nature of the work, and the fact that the place did not have an automatic dishwasher yet, the employee turnover rate for dishwashers was quite high. Sometimes Erika had to do the dishes herself between taking orders and serving. Other times, when it was really busy, she had to bring her kids down to help if they were not in school. That's one of the reasons that neither child wanted to take over the restaurant in later years. It was tiring work.

At one time, it seemed almost impossible to find someone to do dishes. Busboys were easier. They got tips in addition to their hourly wage, so people were more eager to do that job. In order to fill the position, Tasso went down to the local unemployment office and posted a note that they were looking for help. He informed the lady in the office that he was in need of an employee so that she could send them someone when someone became available.

A few days went by and a man was sent from the unemployment office to fill the position. Ron was about forty-five, a native of Illinois and had very few marketable job skills. In his previous job he told Erika that he was 'in charge of the fries' along with his dishwashing duties. She told him that he wouldn't need to do that at Tasso's. The busboys would bring him the dishes, and all he had to do was wash them. The lunch rush came and Ron was hard at work. The problem was that the dishes kept piling up and he seemed to operate at only one speed. Slow. Erika kept going in the back for clean dishes but they weren't ready. She politely asked for some salad dishes and Ron answered "Yes ma'am." Ten minutes later Erika was still waiting. When things really backed up and the cooks had nowhere to put the food, Erika told Ron he could take a break and have some coffee out front. The minute he left, she immediately started washing. By the time Ron returned, there were only some pots and pans for him to clean until the next wave of customers came. Ron only lasted a week until he claimed his back problem was acting up and he would have to quit since the dishes were so heavy. Erika wondered about his work ethic. She assumed that when someone needed to work to survive, one did what was necessary. That's how she was raised.

A few days later, the agency sent another dishwasher named Jim. Jim was about twenty-five, just shy of six feet tall, with a slight build and a pleasant, easy-going personality. He was also African American. It was early morning and there was nothing for Jim to start on right away, so Erika told him to have breakfast or coffee, before he got to working. She and Tasso were very good to their employees. They treated them as equals and the way they themselves would want to be treated. For this reason, most of their employees stayed on with them for many, many years. One of the waitresses and some of the customers were looking at Jim awkwardly. There weren't many African Americans in the area in the early eighties, and a lot of the customers had an early 'southernish' belief system. Being considered minorities themselves in Germany, where they were called 'ouslanders' (outsiders), Erika and her husband didn't share some of their customers' biased beliefs. They felt people were all the same and needed opportunities to better themselves.

"Erika, are you sure you want that guy working here?" asked Jill, a waitress who did a brief stint in the restaurant.

"Yeah, he look like goot boy. Very nice." Erika replied.

She knew a little about American history and remembered how some people behaved towards minorities when she lived in Chicago. It made her sad. (When she had time in later years, Erika liked to watch ***All in the Family*** reruns because it reminded her of some of the customers she met over the years. She doubted whether they would have understood the message of the show).

"I don't know Erika. You never know if you can trust those people." Jill said seeming concerned about their safety.

Erika was a bit more firm in saying,

"He be fine. He only wanne to work just like you en me."

Jim finished his breakfast and went into the kitchen to begin his shift. The breakfast rush came and the dishes kept coming in a steady stream. He did his best to keep up and exhaled heavily as baskets of dirty plates arrived one after the other. When there was a lull after the breakfast rush, Erika proceeded into the kitchen to tell Jim he could take a coffee break. He smiled at her and, as he removed his apron and handed it to her, said "Thanks ma'am but I gotta go. This is white man's work." He left, smiling, and Erika couldn't help but laugh.

Mourning?

Death is a very serious matter among the Greeks. At Greek funerals, friends and relatives, attired in black clothes, wail behind the deceased as they are carried by the men in the family to their final resting place. If you close your eyes, you might think you are at some African tribal ritual with the 'miroloyee', which is the combination of wailing and chanting and screaming of the dead person's name by the women in the family. The only difference is that during a Greek funeral some of the women actually pull their hair out to express their sorrow. Some even throw themselves on the casket. So, naturally, when one of the Tasso's regulars died, Erika prepared for the worst. His name was Fred Peterson and he became a familiar face at Tasso's from day one since he owned a motel only two blocks away and would come in for his eggs and coffee almost every morning before going off to the motel.

It was a typical Wednesday morning when Fred left the restaurant after his usual morning meal. A few hours later, one of the neighbors, Dave, came in with the news.

"Hey, morning Erika." he said with his southern accent.

In later years Erika often wondered how so many of the customers sounded Texan since they were natives of Illinois.

"Hi David. Coffee?"

"Yup. Did you hear the news?"

Erika looked at him puzzled.

"What news?"

Dave looked at her in surprise that she hadn't heard. It was already 11:30am.

"Fred Peterson died this morning."

Erika almost dropped the coffee pot.

"Whaat, he just be here this morning. Oh that too bad, he so nice man."

Dave nodded in agreement.

Erika thought to herself, "Poor Mary Ann. To lose her husband, and he was quite young." Fred was about seventy. While this may seem old to some people, Erika grew up in a village where people usually lived well passed ninety. Dave's words shook her back to reality.

"Funeral's on Wednesday." he informed her.

"Oh.. ok."

Erika couldn't help feeling sad for the man and his widow. Erika told Tasso the news.

"We have to go; he was a good man, here every day." She said to him in Greek. Tasso agreed.

"Do they send wreaths here?" he asked his wife.

"I don't know, I'll ask one of the waitresses what they do."

The morning of the funeral came and Erika arranged for their shifts to be covered. The restaurant was slow that morning anyway since Fred was well known and a lot of Tasso's regulars were going to the service. Erika put on a black dress and pressed Tasso's black suit. She was surprised that the wake wouldn't be held at Fred's home. In Greece, wakes happened at the deceased's home, so that the person can visit it one last time before going to his final residence.

Upon arriving at the funeral parlor, Erika had her tissues ready because she was quite sensitive to funerals. Funerals always brought back bad memories for Erika because when she was ten she had attended the double service of her two siblings who lost their lives to polio within a week of each other. In Greece, it is tradition to dress the unwed who die as brides and grooms since they never make it to the altar, so seeing her two toddler siblings dressed for a wedding made the funeral even more difficult to attend.

Erika and Tasso walked in to the funeral home and heard laughter. They looked at each other totally bewildered. What could possibly be funny at a funeral? Walking around the room looking for the widow, Erika and Tasso greeted many customers. They were chatting, snacking on cakes and cookies and sipping coffee from Styrofoam cups. Erika mused at how lightly these people took death. In a far corner they heard loud laughter. They had found the widow. Erika and Tasso made their way toward the group and, as the people parted, Erika's jaw nearly dropped. Mary Ann (Fred's widow) was wearing a bright green dress with a wide white belt and white shoes. Erika couldn't believe this woman, who was dressed for a party and laughing, had just lost her husband of forty years.

"Oh, Erika, Tasso!" Mary Ann walked toward them with her arms extended. She hugged them both saying, "Oh thank you both so much for coming."

"I'm so sorry." Erika said with a true heartfelt sigh.

"You know, I kept telling him, 'go to the doctor, get your checkups', he never listened to me. It's his own fault." The widow said shaking her head matter-of-factly. Erika and her husband weren't sure what to say.

"Did you get some coffee?" Mary Ann asked with a smile.

Someone else caught her attention, so she hugged and thanked Erika and Tasso again, spun on her heel and was off to tend to her guests. Erika looked at the casket and felt sorry for poor Fred lying there, lifeless, while no one was shedding any tears for him. Not even his wife. As she and Tasso left, Erika couldn't help but think about all the funerals she had attended up to now and the difference between those and this one. She wondered if these people were not on to something. Screaming never brought anyone back to life, and Erika did believe that our souls went to a better place anyway. Maybe celebrating death was the way to go. When the piano started playing show tunes, (supposedly Fred's favorites) Erika had had enough, it was time to go. Weeks later she heard that Mary Ann sold the motel and was on vacation somewhere in Florida.

Mother's Day

Children are everything to Greeks. Parent's lives revolve around their offspring, almost asphyxiatingly so. A lot of the waitresses at Tasso's were in their late teens, so Erika felt like a mother to them and tried to advise them when she could. She was especially fond of one girl, Rosalie, who worked for a short time at Tasso's. Rosalie was of Italian decent and looked it. She had long raven hair, smooth olive skin, a tall and statuesque figure, and was quite funny and boisterous. Rosalie was raised by her father and stepmother and she once told Erika that Tasso reminded her of her own father since they were both Mediterranean and old fashioned as far as their daughters were concerned. Tasso's Restaurant felt very homey to Rosalie.

One afternoon, Rosalie and one of the other waitresses were on the floor and Erika, as usual, was hosting. The lunch rush was approaching so things were picking up fast and everyone was running back and forth taking orders, picking up and serving dishes. Plates were clanging in the kitchen and steady chatter permeated the dining room. Rosalie was standing at the waitress station, smoking a cigarette, and waiting for an order to come up from the kitchen. She was looking out the windows past the eating area when she dropped her cigarette from her fingers and all the color drained from her face. She began shaking uncontrollably and unsteadily ran through the kitchen and out the back door. The cook kept banging the bell twice to signal Rosalie that her order was up and he started cursing in Greek when she didn't pick-up the order. Erika heard him and asked what was wrong.

"Where is that crazy girl!? She better not bring this back to me and tell me it's cold!" he grunted.

Erika scanned left and right for her, but she was nowhere to be found.

"Joan, you see Rosalie anywhere?"

"No hon, and I'm busy."

Erika served Rosalie's order and decided to look in the stock room. As she opened the back door she saw Rosalie sitting on the stairs outside crying and hyperventilating.

"Rosalie, whatse matter?"

"I… I can't go out there!" she sobbed.

Erika was concerned and confused.

"Go where honey, whaaat you talking about?"

Rosalie took some deep breaths and tried to collect herself.

"The lady in the red coat who just came in. I don't want to see her."

Erika still didn't understand.

"Erika, you simply can't tell her that I'm here. She can't know that I'm here."

At that moment Tasso threw the kitchen door open and yelled,

"What you two doing? The place is fool!"

Erika told him they were coming in a moment and he went back inside. Erika went into the dining room where the woman in the red coat was standing by the register.

Erika smiled, *"Ken I help you?"*

"Yes, I'm looking for one of your waitresses, Rosalie." the woman said.

Erika pictured Rosalie on the steps, hysterical. The woman continued,

"I'm her mother and I would like to see her." Erika tried to sound convincing when she said,

"Oh, she no work here no more."

"I was told she has been working here for months." The woman responded in annoyance.

"Ya she work here, but one day she just no show up. I donno where she is."

Erika hoped the woman would leave before Tasso caught on and got more pissed.

"Fine." the woman said as she walked out mumbling.

Erika had to find out what was going on. She served the rest of Rosalie's tables and then went out to get her. Enough time had passed, and it didn't seem like the woman was coming back and by the time Erika went back outside Rosalie had calmed down. As the door opened Rosalie looked earnestly at Erika and asked,

"Is she gone?" Erika nodded and Rosalie let out a heavy sigh. Erika looked at her with concern and asked,

"What's going on? Who was the lady?"

Rosalie's eyes welled up again.

"That was my real Mom."

"Why you don wanne to see her?" Erika asked.

"Because she left me when my parents got divorced. She took my brother with her and left me with my dad. She didn't want me. I only know one Mom, my step-Mom. She raised me like her own child, and this woman abandoned me and didn't even ask about me for years. Now she comes around wanting what? She never cared about me, why should I care what she wants or feels?"

Erika could say nothing. She came from a time and place where parents sacrificed for their children, lived for them. She recalled her own mother wailing hysterically when she lost two children to polio. And here was a woman who chose a man over her own daughter. Erika felt that if the woman could do that to her child, then Rosalie was better off without her.

Later that night, while closing up the restaurant, the phone rang and Erika answered, *"Tasso's."*

"Erika, oh my god, I'm so glad I caught you. I forgot a small pouch under the counter and you have to hide it so Tasso or anyone else doesn't find it." Rosalie sounded hyper.

"What is it?" Erika inquired.

"Oh it's got some lipstick, some cash, and some pot." Rosalie mumbled as if embarrassed to say it out loud to Erika.

Erika, not knowing what pot was, asked her "What?" and Rosalie clarified, "Pot, Mary Jane, marijuana?"

"Oh. Ok I take it en put it away."

After hanging up, Erika didn't want to judge Rosalie, even though she didn't approve of drugs, especially for women; but she figured who was she to criticize.

Celebrate Good Times . . .

Shame is something that Greeks try to avoid at all costs. They live for their name, and families do their best to hide anything that could sully that name. Over the years, Erika and Tasso made friends with many of the families that came to the restaurant. The customers shared their lives with them. They were invited to birthdays, weddings and even funerals. They were surprised though, with one particular invitation. One of the families that came in often was the Davis family. Mr. Davis was a construction worker and his wife worked in a supermarket and their kids were grown. Their daughter lived out of state, they had one son in college and one son, Carl, who lived at home, who was always in and out of trouble. Carl did odd jobs to get by, but unfortunately he was fond of partying so he would squander away what little earnings he made on booze and drugs. Carl's parents still supported him and he still lived at home. The fact that he still lived with his parents didn't faze Erika because Greek kids usually left home only when it was time for them to marry, even if they were in their thirties.

Because of the closeness of the community, like in any small circle of people, news traveled fast. Many of the customers knew each other because they lived in the neighborhood or because they went to Tasso's often and met there. On one Monday at lunchtime Mrs. Davis met her husband at the restaurant and neither one of them looked happy.

"Hi Jim, hi Maureen," Erika greeted them, *"sit anywhere."*

They chose a corner table and all through lunch they sat close together talking to each other in hushed voices. Jim kept cupping his forehead in his hands and shaking his head. Erika knew something was wrong and knew it probably had to do with Carl. She didn't go over to chat with them as usual; they looked like they needed their privacy.

The next day, another regular came in and sat at the counter.

"Hey Erika can I get a coffee?" asked Steve.

"Sure Steve, how are you?" Erika replied as she poured him a cup.

"Okay." Steve smiled.

Erika went about her business and was clearing another spot on the counter that had just vacated when Diane, one of Tasso's longest employees and a good friend to Erika, came over.

"Hi Steve, how's it going?"

"Great." he replied.

"Hey Diane, did you hear about Jim Davis' kid?"

"No, what happened? Is he ok?" Diane was intrigued.

"Looks like Carl got himself into trouble again, but this time it's serious." Steve started to explain.

"They caught him robbin' a convenience store. The stupid kid stole a hundred bucks worth of stuff and the shop owner saw him and called the police. When they came, Carl punched the cop and tried to run, so it looks like he's goin' away for a while because of all his priors." Steve shook his head as he was telling the story.

"Oh wow. Poor Maureen, she must be devastated." Diane said.

Erika was listening to the conversation and her heart went out to the Davis's. She recalled in her mind a time when she was a teenager in the village and one of the village boys was arrested for pushing hashish. His parents moved off of the island to avoid the humiliation.

That evening Erika recounted the story for Tasso. He couldn't believe the kid hit a cop.

"You know, that kid… what am I saying kid? He's

twenty five for Christ's sake… what was he thinking? Imagine how his father must be feeling. They are going to put this in the paper too, for everyone to see." He continued, "Don't say anything to them when they come in unless they bring it up themselves. They probably want the earth to open up and swallow them right now."

"I won't say anything, who do you think I am? You think I don't know how they must feel?"

Erika shook her head at Tasso's advice, like she really had to be told to be discreet when that was one of the first lessons her mother taught her. Erika recalled it in her mind, her mother standing very close in front of her, one hand planted on each of Erika's shoulders and telling her sternly, "You see things, you don't talk. You hear things, you don't repeat them." That was why Erika's mother was the village's trusted confidant.

A few days later, after his court hearing, Carl came into Tasso's for lunch. He seemed to be in good spirits for someone who was going to jail.

"Hey Diane." Carl sounded excited.

"Hi Carl, how you doing?"

"Not too bad. Hey Di, I want your opinion on something." Carl appeared to be holding a garment bag.

"Which do you think will look better?"

He pulled out two cummerbunds and some shoes and smiled while he held them up to himself.

"I'll be wearing a white tux." Carl added.

Erika was walking by as he showed the items.

"Hey Erika."

"Hi Carlo." Erika put a Greek spin on his name. Diane suggested he wear the maroon and she and Erika looked at each other questioningly. Finally, Diane couldn't help herself and she asked,

"What's the occasion Carl, who's getting married?"

"Na, no one. Didn't you hear? I'm having a going away party, and you guys are all invited. It's gonna be great! We rented the pizza pub up the street and I'm gonna leave in a limo. Cool huh?"

Diane asked, "Where are you moving to?"

"Ha ha ha, Joliet." Carl burst into raucous laughter.

"I got nabbed for throwing a punch at a cop, so I gotta go in for two years. No biggie. My parents are all upset, but I asked em' what's the big deal, it's only two years?"

Erika and Diane couldn't believe how lightly Carl was taking this.

"It's gonna be great, you guys should really come, we're even gonna have an Elvis impersonator."

After Carl left, Erika and Diane were discussing the situation.

"My God, those poor people." Erika said.

Diane agreed, "Yeah they don't deserve this."

Erika was still shocked.

"And to hef a party? In my veellage if something like this heppen, we close the doors and windows so nobody know what's heppen."

Diane laughed.

"Diana I'm seerious. We would be so ashamed that we hide it from the other people. He no graduate, ore' get marry. What kineh party this gonne' be? Who gonne' go?"

Diane suggested they attend the party and see for themselves, but Erika knew that Tasso would not go for that.

The day of the party finally came but Carl's parents did not attend, of course. One of the other invited waitresses did go and gave Erika and Diane the scoop the next day. She told them that the pub was full of Carl's friends and cousins. The Elvis impersonator was quite good and Carl, who was a big Elvis fan, got up to sing with him.. Most of the guests got sauced on one type of drink or another. There was dancing and darts and pool and at the end of the night, or rather the wee hours of morning, a white limousine came to take Carl away. As he was getting in, he gave his guests the 'victory' sign with his arms up in the air. He thanked all of his guests for coming and then shouted dramatically,

"Driver, to Joliet!"...... And with that, the limo pulled away.

Heads Up!

Erika's husband felt that to make money, one had to save money. The restaurant was built in the forties, so it was quite old, and over the years many repairs were required. Tasso did many of the repairs himself but he was by far not a craftsman. Tasso knew business and, by his own admission, didn't care to tinker with things. But to save money, he broke down and fixed things himself.

When Erika and her husband expanded the building it cost a bundle. It was the eighties and the economy was not good. Some of the area's biggest steak houses shut down, but Tasso's managed to stay afloat and went on to be successful. However, it didn't come without a price. They lived on very little and enjoyed even less.

The only luxuries they allowed themselves were the occasional trip to visit relatives in Chicago and putting their kids into Greek school, which the kids gladly said they would forego in those tough times.

The first time the roof leaked, Tasso called the contractor, who had built the addition onto the restaurant, and was absolutely furious. The guy came over right away and fixed the problem… supposedly. After a few months the typical Chicago winter snows began and the problem resurfaced. The contractor, of course, was long gone and Erika and Tasso realized that the genius had not built the new roof with the proper slope, so it retained water. One Wednesday morning, after a particularly heavy snow, the dripping began anew. Tasso sent one of the dishwashers up to the roof to remove the snow with a shovel, however with the Chicago snowfalls the problem kept reoccurring. Tasso decided to repair the roof himself. Needless to say, the problem persisted. On dry days it wasn't really a problem, but once the rains came or the snow melted, the people sitting under that spot got their water glasses refilled without even asking.

Every Saturday, a group of mechanics came in at seven am for their usual steak and eggs before they went off to work, and they sat at the same table every week. The six guys were sitting at their table one winter Saturday as always. Halfway into their first cups of coffee, the dripping started. The temperature outside was rising and the snow was beginning to melt… right into their plates. One of them, Bill, noticed a piece of the ceiling tile next to his plate and he called Diane over to tell her that there might be a problem. While Diane was apologizing for the mess, they all heard a crackling noise. They all looked up and within seconds the whole piece of tile came crashing down.

"Holy shit!" said one of the guys. Then they all burst into hysterical laughter. Diane was completely mortified.

"Oh my gosh guys, I'm so sorry. Is everyone ok?" She asked.

They tried to compose themselves.

"Well shit Diane, the thing has been dripping on us for months," he laughed, "it was bound to happen sooner or later."

Erika quickly went over to see what the commotion was about.

"What's heppen?" she asked as she looked from the ceiling to the mess on the table.

Diane recounted the incident for Erika trying to seem surprised in front of the customers. Erika went to get Tasso.

"Hey Tass, roof finally gave." Bill said to Tasso when he walked over.

"Oh man, guys I'm sorry." Tasso said while surveying the damage, hands on hips, lips pursed and barely-contained fury playing in his eyes.

"Guys let's move you over here." Diane said while pickingup the salvageable dishes. "I'll get some new orders for you. It won't take a minute." And she rushed to the kitchen.

Fortunately, the guys had been regulars for years and they all had a good laugh about it instead of bringing a lawsuit against Erika and her husband. After breakfast Tasso put a bus pan on the table and was quite happy with his solution. He figured it would dry up eventually. Erika, in the meantime, called another roofer.

Double Jailhouse Rock

Trouble was not an uncommon occurrence with Tasso's customers. With so many customers and friends, Erika was kind of like a bartender or hairdresser; the customers needed to unload their burdens and, since Erika was trustworthy and a good listener, some of them came in for the sole purpose of talking to her. Erika never told others about the things she heard because of the way she was raised. In her culture, dirty laundry was not to be aired. It was to be locked up in a safe place where no one else could discover it. Because she and Diane (a long time employee and friend) were close, they sometimes discussed, among themselves, what they heard because most of the customers shared their stories with Diane too.

It was another typical Tasso's morning and the regulars were there sipping piping-hot coffee and eating from heaping plates of food, when an old friend came in and sat at the counter. Paul was one of the first people to frequent Tasso's when Erika and her husband took over. This morning, he did not look well. Normally a cheerful and talkative man, today Paul was rather solemn.

"Morning Paul, coffee?" Diane asked.

"Morning Di, yeah I'll have some coffee." He replied.

Erika walked by and greeted Paul also.

"Do you want your usual Paul?" Diane asked as she was already jotting down his usual order.

"Yeah sure, but I don't know if anything's goin' down today." Paul said, not looking away from his coffee cup.

"Rough day already, huh?" Diane joked.

"You could say that." He mumbled.

The morning carried on as usual except that after finishing his breakfast, Paul hung around for quite a long time. He mechanically scanned through the morning paper, but mostly he just sat there, staring at nothing, with a thoughtful look on his face. Erika made some small talk with him but he seemed uninterested and in his own world. Erika's daughter, Kris, came in through the kitchen at that time and Erika assigned her with a task. Now that Kris had a driver's license, she could run errands and take some of the load off of Tasso.

"Do we need anything else from the fruit market?" Erika asked Diane.

"Just some cherries for the ice cream." Diane told her.

Diane knew that since it was one of the kids shopping, they would buy in bulk unlike their father who bought only what they might need.

"I'll be back later." Erika's daughter said as she took the needed money from the cash register before leaving.

Kris was happy at any opportunity to take the car and use her shiny new driver's license. Paul watched her go and, as he drank his sixth cup of coffee, he told Erika,

"You got good kids Erika." Erika laughed.

"Thanks Paul, we like 'em."

"I wish my kids would listen to me like that." He was shaking his head as if unsure.

"Oh Paul, you know kids is kids. They don wanne' do what we say, but sometime they gotta'." Erika replied.

Then it seemed Paul could no longer contain what had been eating away at him all morning.

"Yeah, well right now I got one kid sitting in DuPage County jail and another one in Cook County jail."

Erika was shocked. Diane overheard his confession and walked to where he sat.

"What happened Paul?"

He continued the story.

"Last night I got a call from the DuPage County sheriff saying my son is in lockup for stealing a gallon of wine from a liquor store and do I want to come down to bail him out? An hour passed, and I figured I should go get him, when I got another call. This time it was the Cook County sheriff telling me my daughter's in there for getting into a fight in a bar. Apparently she got into a fight and bit some girl's finger off and spit the blood in her face." He wore a look of total defeat.

"Oh Paul, what you ken do?" Erika asked. She couldn't believe the guys luck.

He went on,

"I sat there last night, next to the phone, wondering what the hell I should do. Who should I go get first? And then I decided I wasn't going to get either of them. A night in jail might shake em' up enough to get them to stop acting like idiots. Teach them a lesson. Maybe if they think I'm not bailing them out anymore, they'll change."

Diane agreed with him.

"Yup, you're right Paul, they need to learn."

Erika couldn't believe what they were saying.

"Oh Paul, you ken't leave the kids in jail. Come on, specially you daughter." She was hoping he would change his mind. *"You gotte' go getem'. Ees worse if they stay there."*

Erika felt sorry for the poor guy, but he had a point, and his kids were adults. Erika wondered where her kids would be in ten years living in this area.

"You're right Erika. But I don't know what to do with them.

"Erika laughingly told him, *"Send 'em to Tasso."*

Paul laughed, paused for a second, as though considering the proposition, and then he got up and left.

Bathroom Backup

Erika's restaurant sat on an acre of land in the western suburbs of Chicago. The area was unincorporated, which means it didn't belong to any of the surrounding villages. One of the drawbacks of not belonging to a village is that the land is not connected to the city's sewer system. On the one hand, the lot had its own water well, which was good. On the other hand, the land had a septic tank that always needed servicing, which was not so good. The original owners of the diner hadn't foreseen the future expansion of the business, and when they sold the place to Erika and her husband it was still a truck stop on Route 20 surrounded by fields.

Summer was a busy time at the restaurant. People

came in to cool off with some iced tea or some other fountain creation. Sunday breakfast was always the busiest time of the week and around eleven am, about the time that the local churches let out, there was often a line at the door. One Sunday in mid-July the thermometer was showing a sweltering ninety-four degrees, the air conditioner was working overtime, the tables were turning over rapidly and Erika was busy distributing menus, giving coffee and working the register. Besides her regular duties, Erika periodically had to check the restrooms to make sure they stayed clean. She was always surprised at how sloppy people could be, especially women. On several occasions she had to call the septic service to deal with things people thought they could flush. Some of the things they found included entire rolls of toilet paper, tampons, diapers, a hand towel, and on one occasion, a child's shoe. To add to the frustration, the sure fire way to know something was in there was when the toilets overflowed on an unsuspecting patron after the culprit was gone. On this particular summer Sunday, everyone was working at warp speed and the bathrooms had to be cleaned three times before noon.

At about twelve-thirty, a handsomely dressed couple came in and were shown to a table in Diane's section. New customers were often given to Diane because she was very personable and chatty and the customers loved her. Besides that, at this time on a

Sunday the only other waitress working was Erika's daughter who was a typical teenager and who would much rather have been working at a music store in the mall like her friends. This being the case, it was best to give the new people to someone who would do their best to get them to come back.

Diane introduced herself and promptly learned that the couple had recently moved to the area and had heard good things about Tasso's. Diane introduced Erika to the newcomers and they made small talk with her while Diane placed their breakfast order. Needless to say, the couple was thrilled with their food. Tasso's lived up to everything they were told; great food, good prices, and friendly service. By her third cup of coffee the lady asked Diane where the restroom was.

"Right by the bar and down the little hallway honey." Diane answered as she pointed in the direction of the bathroom.

The woman got up and made her way to the restroom. The restroom was being occupied, so the lady patiently stood in the hallway waiting for her turn. The occupant opened the door, looked around cautiously and exited looking a bit nervous. The woman entered and noticed some water on the floor but she figured that the previous woman must have splashed water while using the sink. After doing her business, the woman flushed the toilet and proceeded to wash her hands. It was summer so she was wearing crisp white linen pants and open-toed sandals. By the time she noticed, it was too late. The toilet began overflowing and the water sloshed onto the floor, soaking into the cork sole of her sandals and drenching the cuffs of her beautiful pants.

"Oh my God!" she shouted and ran out of the bathroom with the water still chasing her.

"Diane, Diane!! Look at this. Oh God. I don't know what happened!"

Diane was at the counter totaling a bill when she heard the woman's ranting. She immediately went over and Erika was right behind her.

"What happened?" They both asked at the same time.

Diane tried to calm the woman down. The woman was furious.

"I flushed the damn toilet and it overflowed. I was washing my hands and didn't realize... Jesus... I gotta get out of here. Look at my shoes, my pants! I'm in my own filth!"

Exasperated, the woman motioned to her husband to get her things so they could leave. She didn't want to go out into the dining room like that. Erika tried to calm her down, profusely apologizing and offering to reimburse her for her toilet-water soaked clothes. The woman insisted that she had to leave and that's what she did. Erika was humiliated. Needless to say, the couple never came back.

Just Like The Evening News

Erika did the hiring at Tasso's (she left the firing to her husband who was better suited to do that) so when Diane, a long-time employee, suggested they hire Veronica, Erika agreed. Veronica was a sixty year-old tiny spitfire when she arrived at Tasso's. She stayed with them for nearly ten years and worked the weekend morning shift with Diane.

Veronica had a big family comprised of one son, three daughters and a handful of grandchildren. She had been widowed for about five years when Erika first met her. Erika also got to know the whole family since they often came to the restaurant to see their Mom when she was working. The youngest of the daughters, Kathleen, was a good person who tended to make bad choices.

Through Veronica, Erika heard all of Kathleen's troubles. Erika wished she could offer some solutions but these situations usually required professional help. Veronica did the best she could by her kids; she babysat her grandkids, offered financial help when necessary and her home was always open if they needed a place to crash.

One Saturday, during the mid-morning lull, Veronica got a call from her oldest daughter and when she went back to the waitress station she was shaking her head.

"I don't know what I'm going to do with those kids." She said exasperated.

"What's wrong hon?" Diane asked while Erika stood by, equally intrigued.

"My daughter Kathleen decided that she's going to leave her husband again, and asked if she and her kids can come to stay with me. And it's not that she really wants to leave, I've been telling her for years to let go of the bum. But every time she gets ready, when she's at the door, bags in hand, he begs and cries and she goes back. He's out of work again, but won't watch the young one so they don't have to pay for a sitter. And to top it all off, he's started drinking again." Veronica was exhausted after saying all that. "I tell ya, if she doesn't leave him this time, she' on her own."

Veronica waited for their responses.

Erika was saddened by the girl's plight and recalling her early experiences with the drunken neighbors in Chicago said,

"Oh Veronica. You hef to get you daughter and heer kids away from heem soon. You don know what ken heppen if he drink."

Diane agreed and added,

"Honey you take them away from there. Those kids will be in the house alone with him when your daughter is at work. You get them out and you do it fast. Don't take no for an answer."

Veronica nodded in agreement.

"You don't think I know that? Why do you think she left her first husband? Same damn crap."Veronica said.

Her daughter hadn't learned from her first mistake because she had a good heart and was always ready to give people the benefit of the doubt. She was just a bit naïve when it came to her choices in men.

Later that morning Veronica's son John came in for brunch. His hair was slicked back, he was wearing dark sunglasses and his usual look of black pants and a white button down short-sleeved shirt. He looked like something straight out of the fifties. In all the years Erika knew him she had never seen him wearing anything else. He was a product of the early sixties, had Elvis as an idol, and he wasn't going to let his era go, even though it was already the eighties. Erika greeted him and asked him if he wanted coffee.

"Yeah, thanks Erika. Is my Mom around?"

"Yes. She coming now from the kitchen."

Erika walked away to give them their privacy.

"Oh Johnny, good you're here. I didn't know if you were coming today." Veronica kissed her son hello as he sat the counter.

"What's goin' on ma?" he smiled.

"Nothin' good I tell ya'." Veronica gave her son a look that made him realize right away what she was talking about.

Johnny shook his head.

"Now what?"

"Same old, same old honey. When you leave here, go by Kathleen's house and start loading your truck with her stuff. She's finally leavin' that bum."

Veronica gave him some coffee as she told him the news.

"Is she really going to do it this time, or is that loser going to throw bottles at me again, yelling at me to get off his property?" John was remembering the last time he had gone to help his sister leave.

"She says this is it. She's got the kids all packed." His Mom reassured him.

Erika could hear the exchange and wondered to herself 'aren't kids supposed to be less trouble when they became adults?' She and her husband were helping their respective parents with whatever they could but she wouldn't dream of asking her parents for help at this age, especially since she had long established her own household. Johnny left after finishing his breakfast and Veronica gave him a key to her place so that he could help Kathleen settle in. Not even one hour had passed when John came back to Tasso's. Veronica saw him and immediately knew what he was going to say.

"She's staying." said Veronica with a look of defeat.

"That's what she said. Here's your key Mom, better luck next time."

John kissed his Mom and was out the door.

A few weeks later, Veronica was at work when her middle daughter came in to see her.

"Hey kiddo I wasn't expecting you." Said Veronica, happy to see her daughter.

She lived in the city so visits were sparse.

"Erika, I'm going to sit for a moment ok?"

Veronica sat with her daughter at a small table near the waitress station.

"Ma, I'm not here just to visit. I've got to tell you something because I don't know what I can do about it myself." She said very seriously.

"What's wrong dear, are you ok?" Veronica was now concerned about this daughter too, she didn't know how much more she could handle.

"I'm fine Mom, but Michael called me a few days ago to tell me that his step-dad hit Kathleen again. I hadn't realized that there was a first time, but according to him, this wasn't the first time. Mom did you know about this? What are we going to do? I mean, I knew the guy had a drinking problem, but this is going too far."

Veronica answered her daughter as best she could.

"I told your sister to get as far away from that guy as possible. I even sent your brother to help her move into my house. I told her she should leave before she ends up in a hospital."

Veronica added, "I told her that people don't change. He could promise you everything, but it's what he does that counts."

Her daughter agreed and then asked,

"So what are we going to do? He broke up the house too. Michael may be seventeen but he's not big enough, or strong enough, to do anything to protect them."

"I know dear. I'll have to go over there with your brother and pull Kathleen out kicking and screaming."

Veronica wasn't kidding. Besides her grandson, Veronica also had a granddaughter who was only three years-old living in that house. Later that evening Veronica and her other kids got together to have an intervention for Kathleen. Fortunately, with a bruised face, split lip and a broken spirit, Kathleen had no objection to leaving this time. Apparently her drunken husband's behavior had surpassed any other time and she realized that they had to get away for safety's sake. The whole family planned it out together. Veronica would later recount, to Erika and Diane, the horror story of what happened.

Kathleen's husband worked in a factory since he had no real skills and was trained for little else. The family knew his schedule and so they found windows of opportunity to move some things out of the house without his realizing it. Michael was in school during the day and his little half-sister would go to her aunt's house, like she usually did, until Kathleen got off work. They did not say anything to the little girl for fear that she might give away the plan. This was her father after all, and he was nice to her either because she was his daughter or maybe because she was so small.

It was a Sunday and the plan was move Kathleen and her children on Tuesday while the husband went out for the usual drinks with his friends after work. Everything was ready to go. That Sunday was the day that Veronica's worst nightmare came true.

The call came from Kathleen's sister in Chicago. Erika answered, *"Tasso's, ken I halp you?"*

"Can I speak to Diane please?" the caller solemnly asked.

"Sure one minute please," Erika put down the receiver, *"Diane, telephone."* She waved her over.

Diane picked up the phone and after a moment of listening to the caller her mouth went slack, she turned ghostly white and tears welled up and came pouring out of her eyes. Erika noticed her reaction and quickly went over to her, thinking that something had happened to one of her kids or her husband. She could hear Diane on the phone as she approached her.

"Oh my God! Yes... is there anything I can do? Where is Veronica right now? Okay. I'm so sorry." Diane hung up the phone with a trembling hand and immediately had to sit down.

Erika hurriedly asked, *"Diane is everything ok? Are you kids ok?"* Erika tried to gently shake Diane out of her shock.

"Oh gosh Erika, you are not going to believe this. Veronica's son Johnny went to get Kathleen and the kids so they could leave, just like they had arranged," Diane took a shaky breath, "and he found her in her bed room… dead… with her throat slashed. No one else was home. The police are over there right now. Nobody knows what happened." Diane dropped her head into her hands and began sobbing so hard that her entire body shook.

Erika almost lost her balance and fell over. She had never heard anything like this except on the evening news. She couldn't believe it. The story sent a chill through her body and every hair stood on end. Erika was so overwhelmed that she could barely catch her breath for the tears that threatened to come pouring out of her. Veronica's daughter had been killed in a terribly gruesome way. Erika's employee, and good friend, had to see her child slain. Erika and Diane held each other, both weeping.

"Lord have mercy on heer soul and the person who do this. Where is Veronica?"

Diane relayed the information she got from Kathleen's sister.

"She's at Kathleen's house now. She's in shock, she can't even speak. That was the daughter from the city on the phone. It's already one-thirty Erika, I'm gonna go and see if I can do anything for her."

"Of course. You go, I be here until Joan come." Erika encouraged her to go.

She couldn't fathom what Veronica was feeling now and she couldn't even think about it.

The funeral was a week later since the police were still investigating the murder. Erika and Diane arrived at the service together and Erika did her best to console Veronica, but what mother can be comforted at a time like that? Later, Erika and Diane overheard some others talking about the investigation as they went to pay their last respects. To add insult to injury, it wasn't enough that Veronica lost her daughter, but it seemed that one of the people implicated was her grandson.

"Can you believe it?" someone was heard saying. "Apparently he was the beneficiary of her life insurance policy. Michael received fifty thousand dollars, so the police have to consider him as a suspect. They say he wasn't in school that day."

The listeners seemed to find this tidbit of information interesting and crowded closer to hear more. Erika couldn't believe how disrespectful they were being at Veronica's most difficult time.

As the investigation into Kathleen's murder progressed, it was proven that Kathleen's husband was

was the one who took her life so violently. He was sent to prison for twenty-five to life. Kathleen's oldest sister got custody of the three-year-old girl and Michael went off to live on his own at college. Erika had never imagined that she would be so close to such a horrific tragedy in this, the land of opportunity. She prayed that she never would be again.

Signs

Erika's restaurant was on Route 20 and there were a lot of other businesses on the interstate in the 80's. The area didn't become full of subdivisions and fast food restaurants for another decade.

It was a typical Wednesday morning when some young guys, in their early twenties, came in for breakfast. They were not college kids, just some of the neighborhood boys. Two of them were Paul Cramey's sons and they looked a bit hung-over. The waitress went over to give them coffee and take their order and once they finished they went on to chat about their previous evening out. They had apparently been to a local bar and got a bit rowdy and the bouncer, along with the owner, had thrown them out. The guys were not happy about that. Erika could hear the conversation as she was sitting in the booth behind them with a customer, and friend, named Helga Wienhouse, who owned a local real estate company just down the street.

"I can't believe they tossed us out last night man." said Wayne Cramey.

His brother nodded in agreement. Wayne was about nineteen and his brother was twenty. Of course they had used fake identification to get into the bar the previous evening.

"That guy was an asshole." said one of their friends.

"We should go back tonight and get back at 'em." said another.

Erika and Helga overheard the conversation and were shaking their heads.

"Kids." Helga commented.

"Ya, they be foolish sometime." Erika added.

"Well, I've got to go Erika. I'll see you later." Helga got up to leave and Erika said goodbye to her.

As Helga walked past the young men's table she greeted the Cramey boys, "Good morning boys."

They both answered, "Hi Mrs. Wienhouse."

The boys knew her because the previous year she had helped them get out of a lease agreement and saved them from a hefty fine. Twenty minutes later the boys finished their meal and were on their way. They told Erika that their dad would be by later to take care of their bill.

The following Saturday the customers in the

restaurant were buzzing with gossip. Diane was working with Erika and it was around ten am when one of the regulars came in and sat at the counter.

"Morning Erika." Dave said in his southern accent.

"Hi David. You wanne some coffee?" Erika offered.

"Yup." Dave held up his cup.

Diane came back to the counter and greeted him also.

"Hi Dave, what's up?"

"Somethin's up. I just come from Addison and there's police cars all along Lake Street in front of the businesses. Looks like vandals did somethin' last night."

Erika walked over when she heard the word 'police' and asked,

"What you think heppen?"

Diane asked the same but Dave wasn't sure.

"I dunno. I saw some broken signs though."

Half an hour later Dave left and the police arrived. Erika thought they had come in for breakfast but soon learned otherwise.

"Morning ma'am, we'd like to speak to the owner please."

The officers were not any of Erika's regular police clientele.

"I'm the owner, with my husband, but he no here now." Erika replied hoping they would come back when Tasso was around since he understood the language better.

The older of the officers spoke,

"Well ma'am, we'd like to ask you some questions if you're not too busy."

With the advent of cell phones being years away, Erika had no way of finding Tasso to deal with this, and had to oblige. She showed the officers to a booth and offered them something to drink before they began. They accepted some coffee and the questions started. Diane stood close by in case Erika needed anything and she could tell that Erika was nervous.

"Could you tell us what time you close in the evenings ma'am?"

"We close at ten o'clock." Erika responded.

"Do you live far from here ma'am?" the other officer asked.

Erika pointed to the ceiling, *"We live upstairs."*

"Really?" the officer sounded surprised.

They had parked in the front of the lot so they obviously hadn't noticed the apartment above the restaurant.

"So, last night after you closed up, you went upstairs?" the officer continued.

"Yes." Erika didn't know if she should give more details.

"Did you or your husband hear anything strange last night? Cars late at night, the sound of breaking glass, or anything out of the ordinary?"

Erika shrugged and answered,

"No, but the house is back from the street. We don

hear a lot what heppens. The street busy all night."

She wondered if they had noticed that Lake Street was a four lane highway. How could it not have traffic all night? The truth was that, after so many years at this location, no one in the family even noticed the street noise anymore, especially at night.

While the officer was noting her answers, Erika's thirteen-year-old son, George, came in and went straight to his Mom and asked her in Greek, "What's going on? Why are the police here?" Erika told him that she didn't know yet and told him to make himself scarce. So George immediately left with no further questions. Her serious tone was enough for him to understand.

"Was that your son ma'am?"

"Yes, he my boy." Erika said proudly.

"Do you have any other kids Mrs. Tasso?"

"Yes, one daughter." Erika wondered what this was all about.

"And how old is she ma'am?"

"She eleven." Erika was beginning to tire of the interrogation.

As the officer wrote in his notebook, her mind began to wander back to a time in the village when she was about twelve and the police had come to find and arrest a suspected communist. They tore up the neighbors' house and slapped the young man's father around so that he would give up his son's location. Since then, she was quite wary of the police and their power.

The officer's voice jolted her mind back to the present situation.

"Ma'am I don't know if you've heard, but last night some vandals destroyed a lot of property in this area. Specifically, they busted up a whole bunch of signs belonging to some of the local businesses. We noticed that nothing happened to yours."

The officer's statement sounded like a question and Erika didn't quite follow his meaning. Diane's eyes widened as she heard this.

"I don understend." Erika looked questioningly.

"Well, we wanted to know if you had any idea who could have done this? Now, it can't be your kids since they are so young, but you got any thoughts on who might have done this and why they didn't wreck your sign?" the officer asked.

Erika wasn't sure who would do such a thing.

"I don know. We don bother nobody." She shrugged her shoulders because she was actually puzzled herself.

Apparently, the cops read this from her expression and decided to leave.

"Here's our card. If you hear anything, or your husband remembers something about last night, the number to the station is on there and so is my name."

Diane went over to sit with Erika after the police left and Erika let out a sigh.

"Who do you think did it?" Diane asked her with a sly look on her face.

Erika replied, *"I don know Diane. They say our place and one more hef no problem."*

The news of the late night vandals made the local newspapers and the article was asking for any information in connection to the vandalism. A few days later Helga came in for lunch and sat with Erika at a table. Helga immediately asked Erika if she knew what had happened.

"The police came to me and asked me questions because my sign wasn't damaged." Helga said to her.

"Ya they come here too and ask me eef I know who do et. How I know?" Erika asked Helga.

Helga looked around to see if anyone was within earshot.

"Oh Erika, you mean you really don't know who did it?"

Erika gave her a confused look. *"No."*

"Well, I heard around that it was probably the Cramey boys and their friends. Your sign and mine were the only ones not ruined. Don't ask me why they left out ours. I mean, I've been friends with Paul for ages and I helped him buy his house and got the boys out of a jam so maybe that was it. Some other boys their age were talking about it. You know how kids brag about the things they do that they think are 'cool'. I hope for their sake, if it's true, that it doesn't get back to the police. Paul goes through a lot with those kids."

After Helga left, Erika thought about it for a while.

The boys were always very respectful of her and Tasso, but the damage they had done to the local businesses went far beyond a kids prank. Then her mind went back to when they first bought the restaurant and Tasso spoke on Wayne's behalf without even knowing the kid. Apparently, loyalty was just as important here as it was back home.

Mouse in the House

Erika's restaurant sat on one acre of land. Most of it was paved for use as the parking lot and what remained was left as open fields, partly because she and her husband wanted a place for their kids to play when they were little, and partly because of the septic system. Everyone knows that if you live near a field, there are various creatures that will share that field with you since they laid claim to it way before you did. Fortunately, most of Erika's customers realized this too.

On a quiet Monday evening, Erika was hosting and one of the night waitresses was working with her. After nine the place usually cleared out since they closed at ten. This particular evening there was one couple left in the restaurant, Jerry and Sue. They came in every

Monday night for the Salisbury steak dinner special. The waitress, Joan, was cleaning up and refilling sugar and salt dispensers while Erika was tallying up the guest checks.

Erika went over to the couple,

"More coffee guys? How about some pie for desert, ees fresh today, Boston cream."

Jerry and Sue nodded to each other, "Sure Erika, why not?"

Erika told Joan that they were ready for desert and Joan served the pie and went back to her cleaning duties. Erika finished wiping down and straightening the menus, then she took a stroll around the dining room to ensure that everything was ready for the next morning. She was raised to believe that 'cleanliness is half the road to royalty'. It is a Greek proverb that essentially means that even if you are not wealthy, when your house is tidy and in order, you are equal to royalty. She was pleased as she looked around the place. Everything seemed to be fine. Her employees did good work because they all respected Erika and the manner with which she treated them. They also like the fact that she had no problem getting down and dirty when necessary. She washed dishes, cleared tables, cleaned the bathrooms, and vacuumed… whatever needed doing. She never forgot where she came from or acted like she was above menial tasks. Erika felt that any job done honestly was a job to be proud of.

During her rounds, Erika thought she saw something moving in the corner. 'No way' she thought to herself. She made her way to the table in the far left corner of the dining room and as she approached she couldn't believe her eyes. There was a tiny little field mouse walking along the wood paneling that lined the back of the booth. Erika couldn't believe it. The mouse looked like a trapeze artist balancing on a tightrope. It moved along, minding its own business, ignoring Erika. Suddenly Erika realized that it was heading straight for Jerry and Sue's table. Erika went toward it hoping to get it to change directions but, no dice. 'Mickey' as he was later called, stopped in his tracks as though waiting to see what Erika's next move would be. It was a stand-off. There were tables between her and the mouse so Erika could not get close enough to shoo it away in the opposite direction. After a minute-long stare down, Mickey decided that Erika wasn't going to do anything, and proceeded toward the check-out counter. He balanced his way right to Jerry and Sue and disappeared behind the cigarette machine. Erika was humiliated. What would they think? The restaurant was the cleanest in the area and now people would think that they had mice and were dirty. Erika rushed over when she saw that Jerry and Sue had definitely spotted the rodent.

"Oh my gosh guys I'm so sorry about that. I don know where eet come from. Thees first time I see mouse in the place."

Sue laughed, "Oh Erika, it was a baby. It's easy for them to get inside."

Erika couldn't believe their understanding. Back in the village a house with a mouse would have been the talk of the town and the lady of the house would be disgraced.

"But all round the building ees cement. From where eet come in?" Erika added a little naiveté to her voice.

Jerry cleared it up for her.

"Erika, you guys have doors opening and closing here all day. You really think it's hard for mice to get in? You got an acre of field back there."

Jerry continued laughing but then got serious.

"Erika, we all have property around our houses and anyone who tells you they never had mice is lying. You can't avoid it in these parts. Now cockroaches, that's another story. If we ever see those that will be the last time you see us."

They had a good laugh at Erika's embarrassment, paid their check and left. Erika now regretted offering them the desert. She could have avoided all of this if she hadn't.

That night, Erika and Tasso pulled everything that moved away from the walls to see if the mouse was anywhere to be found, with no luck. They set some traps and sticky paper to see what would show, but found nothing days later. They figured however he had gotten in, he must have gotten back out.

They just hoped that he wouldn't come back... with friends.

Restaurant Arrest

Erika felt comfort in the way her husband protected his family and was always a good provider. He knew how to handle people who drank a little too much with dinner, and could talk his way out of any situation. Unfortunately, one time his directness and no-nonsense manner backfired.

Anyone who has been in a restaurant kitchen knows that above the cooking area there is an exhaust hood that sucks up the heat and grease emitted from the cook top. These hoods contain filters that must be cleaned monthly. Tasso's had a contract with a company that came out on the last Thursday of each month to clean and replace the filters. On one Wednesday, during a lull around four, a man came in and approached Erika who was busy inserting the dinner specials into the menus.

"Hi, my name is Don. I'm with Clarke Restaurant Services and I'd like to offer you a free hood cleaning today."

Erika responded that they already had a company to do that but Don persisted.

"I'm sure you do ma'am but there is no obligation to sign with us. We just want you to see our work and maybe when your contract is up you will prefer us."

Erika asked him to wait a minute and she called Tasso to tell him what the guy wanted. Tasso figured it was a free cleaning, so why not take advantage of it.

Erika returned, *"Okay, you go and clean."*

"Great." Don answered and disappeared into the kitchen.

The whole event was forgotten until the last Thursday of that month. It was two-thirty when the service guy from the hood company arrived and Erika was sipping coffee with the night waitress when he showed up. He was about twenty-years-old, maybe 5'9 and quite scrawny. He looked like a little boy in a man's clothes.

"Good afternoon Mrs. Tasso." he greeted Erika.

For all the years Erika could remember, all the people who didn't know them well thought that Tasso was their last name.

"Hi. Ken I halp you?"

Erika couldn't remember what company he was from because a lot of the service people wore the same overalls.

"It's time for the hood cleaning." The young man replied.

Erika answered, *"We don need et thees month. Somebody did et last week."*

The young man's face became distorted and he seemed angry.

"What are you talking about? This is my account; no one comes here but me."

Erika shrugged her shoulders and replied,

"I don know, somebody do et already."

Furious, the man-boy went into the kitchen to see what she was talking about. He came back out and began shouting at to Erika.

"That's a breach of contract and I'm taking my filters and leaving!"

Erika was now a bit agitated herself.

"You don take nothing. You ken't leave the kitchen with no filter!"

"Watch me." The guy said smugly.

Erika quickly went upstairs to her apartment to get her husband. She woke him up from his afternoon nap and explained in Greek what was happening.

"Get up and get downstairs and do something, we can't stay open without the hood in place!"

This was the first time Erika saw her husband get

up so quickly. He ran down to the restaurant to catch the guy taking the last filter to his truck.

"Hey, excuse me." Tasso yelled, *"Young man, wait a minute. What's you doin?"*

"I'm taking our filters Mr. Tasso. You went against the contract and had somebody else clean them, so I can take them."

"Now just a minute. Somebody come and clean them for free, but I no cancel the contract with you so what ees the problem?" Tasso tried to reason with the boy, but was losing patience fast.

With a lot of back and forth, Tasso finally got the young man to put back the filters so the restaurant could keep running that day. Tasso waited while he put them back in place.

"What I owe you?" Tasso asked when the kid was finished.

"Sixty as always. And I hope you understand Mr. Tasso, you can't have anyone come here and do this, we have a contract."

The youngster tried to sound firm.

"Oh ya?" Tasso lifted his eyebrows in surprise at the boy's attitude.

"Now you understend, thees my place and I decide who come to do what. Now you go home."

Tasso tried to leave it at that, but the boy had spunk.

"Now just a minute, you know I can go right back

in there and take those and there ain't a damn thing you could do about it." The boy was yelling now.

Tasso calmly turned around and took a deep breath, *"You got you money, now you can go."*

The boy tried to reiterate his earlier threat but Tasso stopped him.

"You leave my place now and don come back, you got et?"

The young man started to say he would take his property and Tasso lost his patience.

"I tole you once, now I tell you again. Leave my place and don come back. You try to come to take my feelters and I will break you legs, you got et now?"

Tasso didn't touch the kid but he stood so close that the kid was pressed up against his van. He got in and left without another word. Tasso went back inside and informed Erika and all the employees to let him know if the young guy came back while he was upstairs.

The following morning Erika received a call from the filter company. The guy was very direct and just plain threatening.

"So I hear Mr. Tasso is going to do some leg breaking huh?" the man said angrily.

Erika wasn't sure what the man was saying since he was talking so fast, so she called over the waitress, Jen, and handed over the phone. When Jen took the receiver the guy was still talking, she caught the tail end of his conversation.

"You can tell the tough guy that I'll be there at high noon tomorrow and we'll see who is going to break whose bones!"

And with that, he slammed the phone down. Jen went directly to the kitchen with Erika following her.

"Tasso, the company that sent the boy yesterday called and he was pretty mad. He said to tell you that he'd be here tomorrow at 'high noon to see who's gonna break whose legs'." Jen reiterated.

Tasso laughed it off. Erika and Tasso's son, George, was in the kitchen with them and was working with his father that day.

George looked at his parents and asked, "What do you think he's gonna do?"

Tasso gave his son a 'yeah right' look. He was expecting the kid to come back. Little did he know...

At exactly 'high noon', like the guy said on the phone, the owner of the filter company showed up at the restaurant. He threw the door open and blew past Erika and headed straight for the kitchen. Erika knew exactly who he was so she also went into the kitchen but went into the dishwashing area so she could see what would unfold but not seem like she was watching. The man stopped right at the entrance of the kitchen by the swinging doors.

"So, are you tough guy Mr. Tasso? You the one who is gonna break my son's legs?"

He folded his arms across his chest. Tasso was

surprised and George was a bit uneasy. The guy had a shaved head, was about six feet tall and built like a Mack truck. Tasso took a deep breath and exhaled, showing no fear.

"Ya, that's me. Whatchu wannet?"

The man continued angrily.

"I hear you're going to break my boy's bones. So I came here to let you break mine instead."

The tank, with his arms still crossed, started walking towards Tasso.

Tasso stopped what he was doing and answered.

"Ya, I don hef time for thees now, I'm busy. I explain to you employee about the feelter and he don wanne to understend. You still wanne talk, we go outside. I don wanne shouting in my place."

Tasso didn't want to teach his nineteen-year-old son violence, although he did expect it from him. Greek men were tough and never backed down from a challenge. Even if it was a sure loss, they were expected to go down fighting. Around the other side of the wall, Erika was getting worried.

"We're not going anywhere. I'm taking my filters and there's not a fuckin' thing you can do about it, you got it man? Now get out of my way!"

The hulkish creature started walking toward the cooking area. Tasso, who before he was interrupted was cutting a turkey club, was now really pissed. He walked up to the guy and pushed him up against the cooler with one hand and raised his chef's knife to the man's throat with the other. The guy froze. He definitely wasn't expecting this. Tasso was fuming.

"You not gonna take nothing, you gottet? I try nice to tell the boy to go. I pay him and he don wanne to understend. Now you don get it. Get out my place or I cut you throat, alright?"

Even though he towered over Tasso, the guy knew Tasso meant business.

"Now!" Tasso yelled and escorted him out the back door, knife still in hand.

Erika watched all this and knew it was going to be trouble. As the man got in his truck, he began dialing his car phone.

An hour later the police arrived. Apparently that is who the guy called when he got into his truck. Tasso was still in the kitchen and the lunch rush was over but he still had orders to fill.

"Hey Tasso." Sergeant Jim said from the kitchen doorway.

"Hey Jim, what's up?"

Tasso pretended that he didn't know why the police were there. He also figured that since the arresting officers were customers, he might be able to get out of this. In the old country, any acquaintance with pull helped their friends.

"Sorry Tass, but we got a warrant for your arrest. There's a guy pressing charges against you. He said you threatened to kill him with a knife." The sergeant held up the warrant for Tasso to see.

"What?"

Tasso couldn't believe the coward had called the police. If he had taken a shot at him, Tasso would have respected him more.

"Tasso," the other officer was now in the kitchen, "we got to take you in. Sorry man. We'll read you your rights and then we have to go."

Tasso asked his son if he could handle the rest of the orders since he had to leave. Erika came in to see what was happening and Jim actually looked remorseful when he explained to Erika what was going on. In Greek she told Tasso, "I told you, you have to be careful about what you say. Not everyone takes to bullying. How are you going to get out of this now?" Tasso assured her he would be back in a few hours. Jim's partner pulled out his handcuffs and Jim put a hand up to stop him.

"Put them away man, his family is here and there's people in the place. We'll put them on in the car. Tasso you should bring some bail money so we can get you out of there faster."

The police told Erika and her son that they could come and pick up Tasso from DuPage County Jail in about two hours. And with that, they disappeared through the back door so the customers wouldn't realize what was happening. The regulars at the counter, of course, saw everything.

Erika immediately called their lawyer, not saying

many details since she was not quite sure whether in this country what Tasso had done was legal or not. A couple of hours later, Tasso phoned to tell his wife to send one of his kids to come and get him. His daughter, Kris, was home from school by now and her brother filled her in on the events of the day. She drove to the jailhouse to pick up her father and when she walked in Tasso was sitting in the reception area waiting. Trying desperately to resist the urge to laugh out loud, but not one to miss an opportunity for sarcasm, she greeted her father with,

"Hey Tasso. I bet when you imagined this day, our roles were reversed."

Tasso looked up at her, cocked his head in annoyance, and took the car keys from her hands.

About a month later, Tasso's trial came up. His lawyer thought it best that no one testify since Tasso's claim of self-defense would be hard to prove as he seemingly had threatened the man's son prior to the event. He was convicted with aggravated assault with a deadly weapon and received two year's probation.

His kids still tease him about it to this day.

9/11

It has been said that September eleventh touched every person on every corner of the earth. This was certainly true for Erika.

John had been a regular at Tasso's since the early nineties. He was just shy of six feet tall and slender, with blonde wavy hair, an easy smile, and a great sense of humor. John worked as a medical technician but he didn't really like his job. If he was absent from the restaurant for a while, he would walk in and give Erika a big kiss on the cheek upon his return. He started calling Erika 'mama' within days of his introduction to her, and he called Erika's daughter 'The little Greek princess'. Over time, he got very close to the family.

The last time Erika saw John was in August of

that fateful year. He walked in and was visibly elated.

"Hi Mama!" he hugged Erika hello.

John was alone this morning; he usually came in with his friend Kurt. Erika sat with him and chatted. He began excitedly,

"Well, I finished my training and I'm officially an air-steward for American Airlines!" he was beaming with glee.

"Congratulations!" Erika told him.

"But why you wanne to change job?"

"Oh Mama, I was so tired of the job I was doing and I sat and thought about what I really want to do with my life. I really want to travel around the world, but I can't do that without working. So, I decided that the best way to do it is to work for an airline. I love plane trips so, there you go." John explained.

Erika was happy for him. She had never seen him so delighted. Diane heard the news from nearby and congratulated him too.

"That's great John! When's your first flight?"

John responded with enthusiasm.

"I leave this weekend for Tulsa. I'm going to start with some short flights and when I clock the hours it's bon voyage, I'm going international baby! I can't wait. Paris, London and of course Greece Mama! I'm going to go to our country! I can visit Kristalenia."

John was ecstatic.

He ate his breakfast and had to quickly take off to

run some errands. He kissed both Erika and Diane and said goodbye.

"Wish me luck!" he said as he smiled and waved on his way out the door.

While John was away on his first few flights, his friend Kurt occasionally came in and updated Erika on where he was traveling at the time.

"He's very busy." Kurt said on a weekend in late August.

"Yesterday he left for Texas and one day after he returns he's going to Washington. He really seems to enjoy it. The jetlag slows him down a bit, but other than that he says he is having a great time."

Erika chatted a bit more with Kurt and gave her regards for Kurt to relay to John. After Kurt left, Erika was sitting drinking coffee and thinking back to a time when John brought her an autographed picture of a Greek singer. It was on a trip to New York that John had made to visit his parents.

"Hi Mama! Look what I got for you." He grinned as he handed her the picture.

"Oh wow. Where you get thees? Thank you." Erika kissed his cheek.

John recounted the event.

"Last weekend I went to visit my family in New York and I was sitting next to two ladies on the plane. They were speaking in a foreign language so I asked what they were speaking and they said Greek! The woman sitting by the window told me that she was a singer so I told them all about you and the little princess and I asked her for an autograph so I can bring it to you. She had just done a concert in Chicago and she was on her way to New York for another show. She was really friendly. I told her that one day I would visit Greece with you and we would go see her in concert in the home country."

Erika was pulled out of her reverie when the phone rang.

The morning of September eleventh started like any other day. By eight o'clock, Erika was downstairs in Tasso's having coffee before the breakfast rush started. The restaurant had a television in the kitchen where the busboys worked, to help them pass the time. Unfortunately, the busboys mostly watched the Spanish channels so it was a while before Erika or the staff knew what was going on. At 9:01am the first customer came in with the news.

"There's been a terrible accident." Ron told Erika as he sat for his coffee.

"A plane crashed into one of the New York twin towers. I heard it on the radio on my way in."

"What?!" Diane and Erika said almost in unison. Ron continued, "It's not clear yet what's going on."

He picked up the paper and went on with his day. Erika and Diane went straight into the kitchen and immediately changed the channel to a local news station.

Every channel was showing the chaos and

destruction. Erika, along with the cook and busboys watched in utter disbelief as the scene unfolded. It looked like a scene from a movie... a really horrifying movie. The news broadcasts talked in great detail again and again about the crash and speculating about what could have caused it. They panned to people on the sidewalks looking up in horror and sadness at what was surely a freak accident; when the cameras showed a second plane headed straight for the other tower and followed it as it crashed into the building with purpose; people began running in sheer terror, realizing that this was no accident.

The flames from the planes that were embedded in the sides of the buildings were growing higher and more intense. Tiny figures could be seen jumping from the wreckage trying desperately to escape but falling 110 stories to their deaths. Ash was raining down in the streets like Armageddon and time seemed to stand still. It suddenly hit Erika like a ton of bricks; her son was in New Jersey for work that week and he often drove to New York to visit the World Trade Center. She couldn't feel her legs, her bowels turned watery and bile began to rise in her throat. She collected herself and ran upstairs. Tasso was buttoning up his shirt to go to work when Erika threw the door open and frantically searched the phone book. She couldn't remember the cell number by heart time and began sobbing.

"Oh God, give me George's phone number!"

Tasso was baffled.

"What the hell is wrong with you? What's going on?"

Erika turned on the TV in the kitchen and pointed to the screen. Tasso's body went rigid as he stood in shock and watched the scene.

"What the hell…"

"Give me George's number! He is in New Jersey; I have to see if he is okay!"

Tasso tried to calm her down and took the phone from her trembling hands and began dialing. They both waited with baited breath as the phone rang. After what seemed like an eternity, Tasso heard the voicemail, "Hi, this is George. I am unable to answer the phone right now, but if you leave your name and number, I'll get back to you as soon as I can."

Erika kept asking Tasso if George had answered. Tasso hung up and told her it was the voicemail and they should try again in a little while.

"No." Erika said and ripped the phone from his grip and hit redial.

She got voicemail again, hung up and hit the redial button again. Their minds began to wander to the worst when two minutes later the phone rang. Erika frantically picked it up praying to hear her son's voice.

"Hey Mom, turn on the TV."

"Oh my God!" Erika said, choking back tears. "Are you okay?"

"Yeah. I'm outside the building in New Jersey and

we can see the smoke in the sky from here. This is unbelievable." George told his mother.

Erika was crying so hard that she nearly couldn't catch her breath. Her son was okay.

"All the flights are grounded so we are going to have to drive back. I won't be back to Chicago for a few days, but I'm okay. It's a good thing we didn't drive into the city this time."

George told his mother that he was going back into the building to watch the news, said goodbye and hung up. Erika sank to her knees and thanked God for George's well-being and prayed for the souls of all those people who would never again speak to their loved ones. Some days later, when the initial shock and terror had died down, people around Tasso's had gotten back into their usual routine. It was around that time that Diane solemnly handed Erika the newspaper with tears streaming down her face. There, on the front page of the newspaper, was a picture of John. He was wearing his steward uniform and, as always, a great big smile. The caption told a bit about his life and the fact that he had changed careers so that he could 'see the world'. It turned out that John was in the second plane that crashed into the twin towers. Erika wept for John, thinking about how scared he must have been in his final moments. She wept because life was unfair to this young man and to all the others who perished on that dreadful day.

That Sunday, Erika took the day off and went to

church. She lit a candle and prayed for John's soul, and for the thousands of people who died senselessly for the will of a tyrant. Erika would miss her friend.

Tasso Spyratos and his wife, Erato, stand behind the counter at Tasso's Restaurant in Roselle. Next week is the restaurant's 25th anniversary.
Daily Herald Photo/ Scott Sanders

Epilogue

Erika and her husband stayed on at the restaurant for a few more years and celebrated Tasso's Restaurant's 25th anniversary before retiring back to Greece. She really didn't want to go, she had built a life, raised a family and made countless friends that she had hoped would have lasted for all of her life, but that was the plan they had set some forty years back. Erika and her husband returned to their homeland for retirement, right back where they started. Erika's life had come full circle and brought her back to her roots. There were many tears when she left, and she took with her many memories that would last a lifetime. Memories that could only have happened in Erika's America.

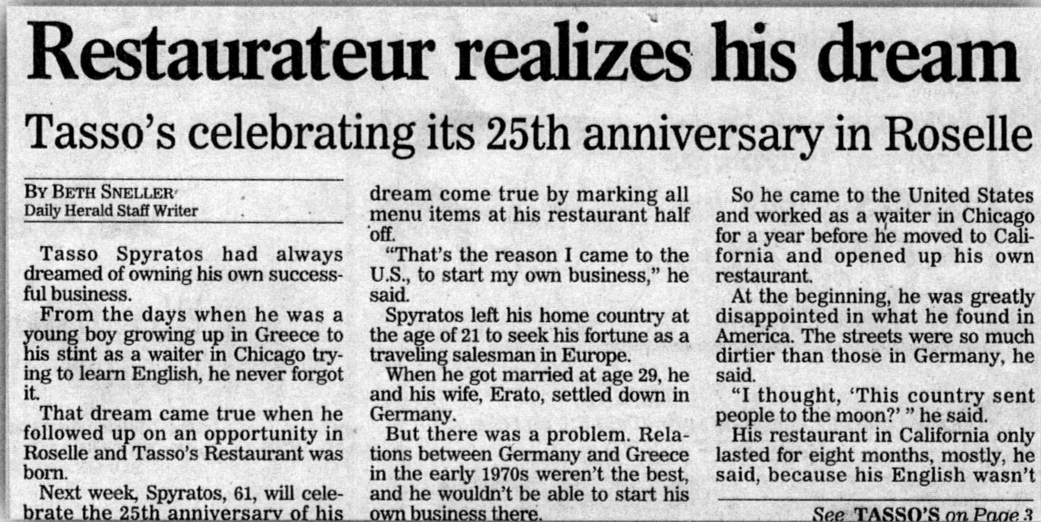

Restaurateur realizes his dream

Tasso's celebrating its 25th anniversary in Roselle

BY BETH SNELLER
Daily Herald Staff Writer

Tasso Spyratos had always dreamed of owning his own successful business.

From the days when he was a young boy growing up in Greece to his stint as a waiter in Chicago trying to learn English, he never forgot it.

That dream came true when he followed up on an opportunity in Roselle and Tasso's Restaurant was born.

Next week, Spyratos, 61, will celebrate the 25th anniversary of his dream come true by marking all menu items at his restaurant half off.

"That's the reason I came to the U.S., to start my own business," he said.

Spyratos left his home country at the age of 21 to seek his fortune as a traveling salesman in Europe.

When he got married at age 29, he and his wife, Erato, settled down in Germany.

But there was a problem. Relations between Germany and Greece in the early 1970s weren't the best, and he wouldn't be able to start his own business there.

So he came to the United States and worked as a waiter in Chicago for a year before he moved to California and opened up his own restaurant.

At the beginning, he was greatly disappointed in what he found in America. The streets were so much dirtier than those in Germany, he said.

"I thought, 'This country sent people to the moon?' " he said.

His restaurant in California only lasted for eight months, mostly, he said, because his English wasn't

See TASSO'S on Page 3

Hello Ericka & Tasso

July 9 '03

We have been in several times & did not see you. The other day we asked the waitress where you were, as another gentleman was pouring coffee.

She explained you were still here, but not working!!

It sounds like "retirement" is your plan?? Will you return to Grece permenently?

What ever your future holds, George & I wish you the very best of health & happiness. You both are wonderful people & we treasure our time spend with you and the kindness you showed to us.

LOVE, Diane & George

Home...

Sweet Home......

ND - #0179 - 060826 - C0 - 216/138/14 - PB - 9781784560973 - Gloss Lamination